Good Housekeeping
Cookery Club

Soups & STARTERS

Louise Pickford

EBURY PRESS
LONDON

First published 1995

1 3 5 7 9 10 8 6 4 2

First published in the United Kingdom in 1995 by
Ebury Press, Random House, 20 Vauxhall Bridge Road, London SW1V 2SA

Random House Australia (Pty) Limited
20 Alfred Street, Milsons Point, Sydney,
New South Wales 2061, Australia

Random House New Zealand Limited
18 Poland Road, Glenfield,
Auckland 10, New Zealand

Random House South Africa (Pty) Limited
PO Box 337, Bergvlei, South Africa

Random House UK Limited Reg. No. 954009

A CIP catalogue record for this book is available from the British Library.

Managing Editor: JANET ILLSLEY
Design: SARA KIDD
Special Photography: GUS FILGATE
Food Stylist: LOUISE PICKFORD
Photographic Stylist: JANE MC LEISH
Techniques Photography: KARL ADAMSON
Food Techniques Stylist: ANGELA KINGSBURY
Recipe Testing: EMMA-LEE GOW

ISBN 0 09 179094 8

Typeset in Gill Sans by Textype Typesetters, Cambridge
Colour Separations by Magnacraft, London
Printed and bound in Italy by New Interlitho Italia S.p.a., Milan

CONTENTS

COOKERY NOTES

- Both metric and imperial measures are given for the recipes. Follow either metric or imperial throughout as they are not interchangeable.
- All spoon measures are level unless otherwise stated. Sets of measuring spoons are available in both metric and imperial for accurate measurement of small quantities.
- Ovens should be preheated to the specified temperature. Grills should also be preheated. The cooking times given in the recipes assume that this has been done.

- Where a stage is specified in brackets under freezing instructions, the dish should be frozen at the end of that stage.
- Size 2 eggs should be used except where otherwise specified. Free-range eggs are recommended.
- Use freshly ground black pepper and sea salt unless otherwise specified.
- Use fresh rather than dried herbs unless dried herbs are suggested in the recipe.
- Stocks should be freshly made if possible. Alternatively buy ready-made stocks or use good quality stock cubes.

INTRODUCTION

Gathering friends and family together for any meal is a celebration of both food and conversation and, whether you are planning a formal or informal dinner, getting the meal off to a good start is vital, not only for the cook's confidence but also for the general atmosphere of the occasion. The recipes in this book are designed to ensure that success, with a diverse collection of exciting and inspirational dishes.

If your mind tends to go completely blank when you are planning a meal and you can't think of anything new to cook, use the recipes in this book as a guide. If you have already chosen a main course, pick a soup or starter that will complement this. Of course there really are no hard and fast rules – we all have our own preferences – but it is generally wise to avoid following a fish starter with a fish main course or a meat starter with meat. Variety is important and there is certainly no lack of it in the following chapters.

Forward planning is essential for the success of your meal and here are a few tips to set you on your way. Always think about the season and buy produce that will be at its best at the particular time of year. Asparagus out of season has often travelled a long way – think how you feel with jet lag! It will be hugely expensive and the flavour will be disappointing.

I can't emphasise enough the importance of seasonal eating which sadly seems to be disappearing from our lives. If you have the time and a handy local market, buy your fresh produce there; the fruit and vegetables will be those that are in season and often grown locally rather than imported, with the added incentive that many will be cheaper than their counterparts in the supermarket.

Who you are inviting to dinner is important too: check that everyone will eat what you're planning. Are there any vegetarians coming? If so are they strict or do they eat fish? If you want to serve a dish with chicken livers, check that all your guests eat offal.

Once you've decided on your meal, it should be plain sailing. Most of the recipes in this book are quick and easy to prepare, and many – particularly the soups – can be prepared ahead.

Soups are ideal starters as they are always popular. I have divided them into two chapters: winter and summer soups. The former are generally more hearty and wholesome – perfect for warming away those winter blues – and substantial enough to serve fewer people as a meal in themselves, if you provide plenty of crusty bread. The summer soups are lighter and more refreshing as the time of year demands.

The secret of a successful soup is invariably a well-flavoured homemade stock, so it's well worth using the recipes on the following pages to make your own stocks. Don't forget that your stock will only be as good as the quality of the ingredients used to make it. You can't make a silk purse from a sow's ear – in the same way you can't produce a tasty stock with old limp vegetables! Buy the freshest looking produce you can. If you are really short of time, use one of the 'fresh' stock products now available from the chilled delicatessen cabinets in larger supermarkets.

The starter dishes are also divided into two chapters – hot and cold starters. These dishes are more year-round although, as with the soups, you may decide that a cold starter is more appropriate in the summer months.

All four chapters contain a diverse selection of meat, fish and vegetable based recipes so there is plenty of choice for everyone. For so many of us who enjoy cooking and entertaining, time is at a premium. The majority of the recipes in the following chapters are therefore simple and quick. Many of them can be prepared and cooked at the end of a day's work – making it possible to entertain friends regularly with the minimum of time and effort, and maximum enjoyment.

STOCKS

A good homemade stock forms the basis of most of the soups, so use the following chicken, vegetable and fish stock recipes as required. If you have time, make up a batch of whichever stock(s) you are most likely to need and freeze in convenient quantities, ready to use at a later date. Don't forget to allow plenty of time for the stock to defrost at room temperature, about 4 hours. Alternatively remove from the freezer the day before required and defrost overnight in the refrigerator.

VEGETABLE STOCK

2 onions, peeled
2 large potatoes, peeled
2 large leeks, trimmed
4 carrots, peeled
2 celery sticks
4 ripe tomatoes, chopped
125 g (4 oz) mushrooms, chopped
60 ml (4 tbsp) olive oil
2 garlic cloves, peeled
150 ml ($\frac{1}{4}$ pint) dry white wine
50 g (2 oz) red lentils
1 bouquet garni
10 ml (2 tsp) sea salt
1.75 litres (3 pints) water

MAKES 1.5 LITRES (2$\frac{1}{2}$ PINTS)

1. Roughly chop the onions. Cut the potatoes into cubes. Slice the leeks, carrots and celery. Chop the tomatoes and mushrooms.

2. Heat the oil in a large saucepan, add the garlic, onions and leeks and fry for 10 minutes. Add the carrots, potatoes and celery; fry for 10 minutes until softened but not coloured.

3. Add the wine and boil rapidly for 5 minutes until almost completely reduced. Add all the remaining ingredients. Bring to the boil, cover and simmer for 1 hour. Strain the stock through a fine sieve and cool, or simmer partly covered to reduce, for a more intense flavour. Cool and refrigerate for up to 3 days.

FISH STOCK

Most fishmongers will give you fish heads and trimmings, especially if you buy fish regularly from them, or they will sell them cheaply. Fish stocks that are made with heads should only be simmered for 30 minutes as they can turn bitter and unpleasant with longer cooking. Some supermarkets sell ready-made fish stocks in the chilled cabinet alongside the fish. Use stock cubes only as a last resort as they tend to be rather salty and not very fishy!

900 g (2 lb) fish trimmings
2 large carrots, peeled
1 onion, peeled
2 celery sticks
2 leeks, trimmed
2 garlic cloves, peeled
900 ml (1$\frac{1}{2}$ pints) dry white wine
45 ml (3 tbsp) white wine vinegar
2 bay leaves
4 fresh thyme sprigs
4 fresh parsley sprigs
6 white peppercorns
5 ml (1 tsp) sea salt
900 ml (1$\frac{1}{2}$ pints) water

MAKES 900 ML (1$\frac{1}{2}$ PINTS)

1. Wash and dry the fish trimmings. Chop the carrots and onion; slice the celery and leeks. Place in a large saucepan with remaining ingredients.

2. Bring to the boil, skim the surface and simmer, covered, for 30 minutes.

3. Strain the stock through a fine sieve into a clean pan and return to the boil. Simmer, uncovered, for a further 15 minutes or until the liquid is reduced by half. Allow the stock to cool. Refrigerate for up to 3 days.

CHICKEN STOCK

You will need to buy a boiling chicken to make a tasty stock; the best option is to ask your butcher as supermarket chickens are not usually suitable for boiling. This recipe yields a richly flavoured stock, and you can reserve the cooked chicken and vegetables for a separate dish.

1 large boiling chicken, about 2 kg (4½ lb)
2 onions, peeled
4 carrots, peeled
2 celery sticks
4 ripe tomatoes, chopped
2 leeks, trimmed
2 garlic cloves, peeled
4 fresh parsley sprigs
1 bouquet garni
10 ml (2 tsp) sea salt
10 ml (2 tsp) sugar

MAKES 1.5 LITRES (2½ PINTS)

1. Wash and dry the chicken thoroughly, inside and out, and place in a large saucepan. Chop the onions, carrots, celery and tomatoes; slice the leeks. Add the vegetables to the chicken with the remaining ingredients.

2. Pour in sufficient cold water to cover the chicken. Bring slowly to the boil, skim the surface and simmer, covered, for 3 hours.

3. Remove the vegetables and chicken with a slotted spoon. Allow to cool and refrigerate overnight.

4. Carefully skim off the congealed layer of fat from the surface of the stock. Use as required, storing it in the refrigerator for up to 3 days.

GARNISHES

Most of the soup recipes include a complementary garnish, but there are many alternatives. Sometimes you may prefer a more simple garnish, or something a little more substantial to add an extra element. The following ideas are suitable for most soups.

CREAM GARNISHES

Spoon a little cream into the centre of the soup and, using a cocktail stick, swirl the cream to make a delicate feather pattern.

HERB GARNISHES

Finely snip over a few chives or tear and scatter over a few leaves, such as parsley, basil, coriander or mint. Or garnish the soup with a sprig of herbs.

CHEESE GARNISHES

Grate some Cheddar or Gruyère and sprinkle onto each soup portion. Or top each serving with a few shavings of Parmesan or Pecorino cheese.

Lightly whip a little double cream until it just holds its shape and spoon onto the soup. Sprinkle over a little paprika, cayenne pepper or nutmeg, depending on the flavour of the soup. Alternatively, combine a little Greek yogurt or cream with 15 ml (1 tbsp) chopped fresh mint coriander or chives. Spoon a little into the centre of each soup portion.

PESTO GARNISH

Spoon a little pesto into the centre of each soup. Basil pesto is good with chunky vegetable soups (see page 42); olive paste provides the perfect partner for a tomato soup (see page 44); rocket pesto (see page 40) is delicious stirred into potato or root vegetable soups.

Lightly toast 4 thin slices French stick on one side, sprinkle the untoasted side with plenty of grated cheese and grill until melted and golden. Use to garnish each soup portion.

BREAD GARNISHES

CROÛTONS are a classic garnish.

1. Remove the crusts from 4 thick slices of bread and cut the bread into cubes.

2. Heat a 1 cm (½ inch) depth of vegetable oil in a frying pan and, when hot, add the bread. Stir-fry over a medium heat until evenly browned.

3. Remove from the pan and drain on kitchen paper.

MELBA TOAST is more of a serving suggestion than a garnish, and goes well with many soups.

1. Take 4 thin slices of bread and remove the crusts, forming squares. Grill lightly on both sides until golden.

2. Cool slightly, then slice each piece horizontally into two, and then diagonally into triangles.

3. Grill on both sides until golden and curled up at the edges.

BRUSCHETTA is an Italian garlic and oil dressed bread which is delicious with almost any soup. It can be used to top the soup or placed in the bowl and the soup poured on top.

1. Grill 4 thick slices of slightly stale bread lightly on both sides.

2. Immediately rub the bread all over with a whole peeled garlic clove.

3. Drizzle with a little fruity extra-virgin olive oil. Serve at once.

CITRUS GARNISHES

TANGY CITRUS BUTTER: A few slices of one of these makes a tasty garnish.

CITRUS SLICES are suitable garnishes for creamy soups, as they cut through the richness.

CITRUS OIL makes a flavoursome soup garnish and it's easy to make your own version.

1. Finely grate a little lemon, orange or lime rind and blend with some softened butter.

1. Peel a small orange, removing all peel and white pith.

1. Peel 2 strips of rind from an orange, lemon or lime and bruise lightly with a rolling pin.

2. Form into a log shape, wrap in greaseproof paper or foil and chill until firm.

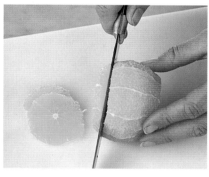

2. Slice crosswise into rounds, then halve each round to form semi-circles.

2. Place in a small jar with enough olive oil to cover. Refrigerate for up to 5 days.

3. Thinly slice the butter and top each soup with several slices.

3. Serve a couple of orange slices on each portion of soup.

3. Strain out the peel and drizzle the infused oil over each portion of soup.

CURRIED MUSSEL SOUP

It is best to buy mussels several hours before cooking and soak them in cold water with a little wholemeal flour or oatmeal added to the water. This helps clean out their digestive systems and rids them of excess grit. After soaking, scrub the mussels to remove the grit and pull out the "beards" that remain attached to the shells. Discard any that are cracked or wide open.

SERVES 4

900 g (2 lb) fresh mussels
pinch of saffron strands
600 ml (1 pint) fish or
   vegetable stock
   (see page 5)
2 small leeks, trimmed
30 ml (2 tbsp) olive oil
1 garlic clove, crushed
30 ml (2 tbsp) mild curry
   paste
2.5 ml ($\frac{1}{2}$ tsp) mustard
   powder
150 ml ($\frac{1}{4}$ pint) dry cider
150 ml ($\frac{1}{4}$ pint) double
   cream
15 ml (1 tbsp) chopped fresh
   chervil or parsley
salt and pepper

PREPARATION TIME
20 minutes
COOKING TIME
20 minutes
FREEZING
Not suitable

320 CALS PER SERVING

1. Preheat the oven to its lowest setting. Clean the mussels thoroughly under cold running water, removing their beards and discarding any with open or cracked shells. Put the saffron strands in a bowl. Heat the stock, pour over the saffron and leave to soak for 10 minutes.

2. Meanwhile, slice the leeks. Heat the oil in a large saucepan, add the garlic and leeks and fry gently for 5 minutes until soft but not coloured. Stir in the curry paste, mustard powder and cider. Boil rapidly until the cider is almost completely reduced.

3. Add the mussels, stir once and pour in the saffron stock. Bring to the boil, cover and simmer gently for 6-8 minutes until the mussels have opened. Discard any that remain closed.

4. Carefully strain the liquid through a fine sieve into a clean saucepan. Transfer the mussels to warmed soup bowls and keep warm in the oven.

5. Bring the liquid to a simmer and whisk in the cream and chervil or parsley. Bring to the boil and boil steadily for 5 minutes. Season with salt and pepper to taste and pour immediately over the mussels. Serve at once.

VARIATION

For a coconut curry soup, replace the double cream with the same amount of coconut milk. Bring to a gentle simmer and immediately pour over the mussels.

TECHNIQUE

Scrub the mussels thoroughly under cold running water and pull away the beard from each shell.

SMOKED FISH CHOWDER

I have used all milk to make a rich stock for this attractive chowder but if you prefer a lighter soup you could use half milk and half vegetable or fish stock (see pages 5-6). I was once served a fish chowder in Seattle – in a hollowed-out crusty bread roll. It looked so intriguing as it was set down in front of me and tasted so delicious, that I have included it as a variation here.

SERVES 4-6

**450 g (1 lb) skinless smoked
    haddock fillet**
1.2 litres (2 pints) milk
2 onions, peeled
2 celery sticks, trimmed
1 bay leaf
2 fresh parsley sprigs
6 white peppercorns
25 g (1 oz) unsalted butter
1 garlic clove, crushed
150 ml (¼ pint) dry sherry
**125 g (4 oz) piece smoked
    ham**
225 g (8 oz) sweet potato
**125 g (4 oz) fresh or frozen
    sweetcorn kernels
    (see note)**
**125 g (4 oz) smoked salmon,
    sliced**
TO SERVE
croûtons (see page 8)
chopped parsley, to garnish

PREPARATION TIME
20 minutes, plus cooling
COOKING TIME
30 minutes
FREEZING
Not suitable

560-70 CALS PER SERVING

1. Place the smoked haddock in a frying pan with the milk. Finely chop the onions; slice the celery. Add half of the chopped onion to the pan with the celery, bay leaf, parsley sprigs and peppercorns. Bring slowly to the boil, simmer for 1 minute and then turn off the heat. Allow to cool. Carefully remove the fish from the pan and flake into pieces; set aside. Strain the milk and reserve.

2. Melt the butter in a large pan and fry the remaining onion and garlic for 5 minutes until softened but not coloured. Add the sherry and boil rapidly for 5 minutes until almost completely reduced.

3. Meanwhile chop the ham; peel and dice the sweet potato. Add to the pan with the fresh sweetcorn kernels, if using, and reserved poaching liquid. Bring to the boil, cover and simmer over a low heat for 20 minutes. (If using frozen sweetcorn add to the pan after 10 minutes.)

4. Stir in the flaked haddock and smoked salmon, and heat through for 3-4 minutes without boiling. Serve topped with croûtons and chopped parsley.

NOTE: You will need 1 corn cob for this quantity of kernels. Strip the corn kernels from the cob, using a sharp knife.

VARIATION

Cut the tops from 4-6 large brown crusty rolls and scoop out most of the bread inside, leaving 1 cm (½ inch) thick shells. Bake the rolls and tops in a pre-heated oven at 190°C (375°F) Mark 5 for 10-15 minutes until crisp. Sit the rolls in warmed soup bowls and spoon in the chowder. Replace the lids and serve at once.

TECHNIQUE

Carefully divide the poached smoked haddock into flakes.

THAI SHELLFISH SOUP

With many of the exotic ingredients used in oriental dishes now readily available in our stores, authentic Thai dishes are far easier to achieve. Red curry paste provides the main flavouring for this tasty soup. For optimum flavour, make your own paste (see below); use the remainder in other Thai dishes, such as curries and stir-fries. Alternatively you can buy jars of ready-made Thai red curry paste.

SERVES 4

8 large raw prawns in shells
20 fresh mussels
4-8 small squid, cleaned
4 large cooked crab claws
900 ml (1½ pints) fish or
    vegetable stock (see
    page 5-6)
15 ml (1 tbsp) groundnut or
    sunflower oil
15-30 ml (1-2 tbsp) Thai red
    curry paste (see below)
300 ml (½ pint) coconut
    milk
30 ml (2 tbsp) light soy
    sauce
salt and pepper
coriander leaves, to garnish

PREPARATION TIME
30 minutes
COOKING TIME
1 hour
FREEZING
Not suitable

350 CALS PER SERVING

1. Prepare the shellfish. Peel the prawns and place the heads and shells in a large saucepan. Scrub the mussels thoroughly in plenty of cold water and remove the beards. Discard any mussels which do not close when tapped firmly. Slice the squid into rings and halve the tentacles, if large. Separate the crab claws at the joints and crack the shells slightly with a mallet or nut crackers. Set all the shellfish aside.

2. Add the stock to the prawn shells, bring to the boil, cover the pan and simmer gently for 30 minutes. Strain and reserve the stock.

3. Meanwhile, place the mussels in a large saucepan with a little water. Cover with a tight-fitting lid and cook over a high heat for 3 minutes until the shells are steamed open. Drain the mussels and discard any that remain closed. Refresh the mussels immediately under cold running water and set aside.

4. Heat the oil in a clean pan, add the Thai curry paste and fry, stirring, over a gentle heat for 2 minutes. Stir in the reserved prawn stock, coconut milk, and soy sauce. Bring to the boil, cover and simmer gently for 20 minutes.

5. Add the prawns and crab claws to the soup. Simmer for 5 minutes, then add the squid and mussels. Heat through for a further 3-4 minutes and check the seasoning. Serve at once, garnished with the coriander leaves.

THAI RED CURRY PASTE: To make your own version you will need 8 dried red chillies, seeded; 8 coriander roots, scrubbed; 2.5 cm (1 inch) piece fresh root ginger, peeled and chopped; 4 kaffir lime leaves, shredded; 2 lemon grass stalks, peeled and chopped; 4 garlic cloves, peeled and chopped; 2 shallots, peeled and chopped; 5 ml (1 tsp) black pepper; and 15 ml (1 tbsp) sunflower oil. Place all the ingredients in a blender or food processor and work to a smooth paste. Store in a screw-topped jar in the refrigerator for up to 1 week.

NOTE: Cracking the crab claws prior to cooking makes getting into the flesh easier. So don't forget the finger bowls!

TECHNIQUE

Separate the crab claws at the joints and crack the shells slightly.

OXTAIL AND ONION SOUP WITH CAMEMBERT TOASTS

The rich depth of flavour derived from the oxtail makes the advance preparation of the stock for this soup well worthwhile. Be sure to get your butcher to cut the oxtail into chunks for you as the bone that runs through the centre is very hard indeed. Garlic and Camembert topped croûtons are an unusual garnish, but the creamy, gooey texture of the melted cheese is quite wonderful.

SERVES 4

900 g (2 lb) oxtail, in chunks
    (see above)
I small leek, trimmed
2 carrots, peeled
2 celery sticks
I bouquet garni
1.75 litres (3 pints) water
I large head of garlic
30 ml (2 tbsp) olive oil
900 g (2 lb) red onions
50 g (2 oz) unsalted butter
15 ml (1 tbsp) chopped fresh
    thyme
5 ml (1 tsp) sugar
5 ml (1 tsp) salt
150 ml (¼ pint) red wine
pepper
TO SERVE
125 g (4 oz) Camembert
    cheese
4 slices French stick

PREPARATION TIME
30 minutes, plus overnight chilling
COOKING TIME
2¾ hours
FREEZING
Suitable: Without toasts

605-405 CALS PER SERVING

1. Wash the oxtail chunks and pat dry. Chop the leek, carrots and celery, and place in a large pan with the oxtail, bouquet garni and water. Bring to the boil, skim the surface to remove any scum, cover and simmer for 2 hours. Strain the stock into a clean pan. Leave to cool and chill overnight.

2. The following day, preheat the oven to 200°C (400°F) Mark 6. Cut a thin slice from the top of the garlic and sit on a double piece of foil. Drizzle over the oil and fold over the foil to seal in the garlic. Bake for 45-50 minutes until the garlic cloves are tender. Remove from the oven and leave to cool slightly.

3. Meanwhile, remove the fat from the surface of the stock. Bring the stock to the boil and simmer to reduce to about 900 ml (1½ pints).

4. Peel and thinly slice the onions. Melt the butter in a large heavy-based pan, add the onions and fry over a medium heat for 20-25 minutes until caramelised. Stir in the thyme, sugar and salt and continue to fry for a further 5 minutes.

5. Pour in the red wine and boil rapidly until well reduced, then add the stock. Bring to the boil, cover and simmer for

20 minutes. Season with salt and pepper to taste and keep warm.

6. Preheat the grill. Squeeze the garlic cloves from their skins and mash to a paste. Cut the Camembert into thin slices. Lightly toast the French stick slices on one side, then spread the garlic paste over the untoasted side and top each one with a slice of Camembert. Grill for 1-2 minutes until bubbling and golden.

7. Divide the soup between warmed serving bowls and top with the toasts. Serve at once.

TECHNIQUE

Squeeze out the softened garlic cloves from their skins and spread onto the slices of French bread.

BEAN, CABBAGE AND CHORIZO SOUP

This hearty winter soup is based on two classic Mediterranean soups from different countries – the Spanish *Caldo Verde* and the Italian *Ribollita*. Both are thick with cabbage and beans, and include a meat of some sort. I like to add a spicy chorizo or other Spanish sausage for a richer flavour.

SERVES 4

125 g (4 oz) dried haricot
   beans, soaked overnight in
   cold water
125 g (4 oz) piece pancetta
   or bacon
2 onions
4 garlic cloves, peeled
1 fresh rosemary sprig
6 black peppercorns
1.5 litres (2½ pints) water
225 g (8 oz) Savoy cabbage
225 g (8 oz) spicy chorizo
   sausage
30 ml (2 tbsp) olive oil
15 ml (1 tbsp) chopped fresh
   rosemary
salt and pepper
extra-virgin olive oil, to
   serve

PREPARATION TIME
15 minutes, plus overnight
soaking
COOKING TIME
1¼ hours
FREEZING
Suitable

525 CALS PER SERVING

1. Drain the beans, rinse and place in a large pan with the pancetta or bacon. Peel and chop the onions. Place half the chopped onion and two of the garlic cloves on a piece of muslin with the rosemary sprig and peppercorns, then tie the muslin into a bag with string.

2. Add the bouquet garni to the pan with the water. Bring to the boil and boil rapidly for 10 minutes, then lower the heat, cover and simmer gently for 45 minutes or until the beans are tender. Discard the pancetta and muslin bag.

3. Meanwhile, roughly shred the cabbage; slice the chorizo; chop the remaining garlic. Heat the oil in a clean pan and fry the chopped garlic with the rosemary and remaining onion for 5 minutes until lightly golden. Add the sausage and continue to fry for a further 5 minutes. Stir into the cooked beans with the cabbage, bring to the boil and cook for a further 15-20 minutes until the sausage and cabbage are cooked. Season with salt and pepper to taste.

4. Transfer the soup to warmed bowls and drizzle with extra-virgin olive oil. Serve at once, with crusty bread.

VARIATIONS

Use cannellini beans instead of haricot beans; soak and cook as above. If chorizo is unavailable, replace with another type of spicy sausage.

TECHNIQUE

Place 1 onion, chopped; 2 garlic cloves, a rosemary sprig and 6 black peppercorns on a square of muslin and tie to form a bag.

BEETROOT SOUP WITH HORSERADISH DUMPLINGS

This beetroot soup is similar to a Russian *Borscht* which is traditionally made with beetroot, cabbage and potatoes in a beef stock. Here the soup is served with light fluffy dumplings and slivers of beef fillet.

SERVES 4-6

125 g (4 oz) beef fillet
1 onion
1 garlic clove
450 g (1 lb) cooked beetroot in natural juice
25 g (1 oz) butter
grated rind and juice of 1 lemon
15 ml (1 tbsp) chopped fresh thyme
1.2 litres (2 pints) beef consommé (see note)
175 g (6 oz) white cabbage
225 g (8 oz) potatoes
salt and pepper
DUMPLINGS
75 g (3 oz) self-raising flour
2.5 ml ($\frac{1}{2}$ tsp) salt
50 g (2 oz) beef suet
30 ml (2 tbsp) chopped fresh chives
30 ml (2 tbsp) freshly grated horseradish
60-75 ml (4-5 tbsp) water

PREPARATION TIME
15 minutes
COOKING TIME
1-1$\frac{1}{4}$ hours
FREEZING
Suitable: Without dumplings and beef

375-250 CALS PER SERVING

1. Place the beef fillet in the freezer for 30 minutes to firm up (to make slicing easier).

2. Meanwhile, peel and slice the onion; peel and chop the garlic. Chop the beetroot. Melt the butter in a large saucepan, add the onion, garlic, lemon rind, thyme and beetroot and fry for 10 minutes until golden. Add the consommé and lemon juice, bring to the boil, cover and simmer for 30 minutes.

3. Meanwhile, make the dumplings. Sift the flour into a bowl and stir in the salt, suet, chives and horseradish until evenly combined. Gradually work in enough of the water to form a soft dough, then shape into 12 small balls.

4. Thinly shred the cabbage; peel and cube the potatoes. Add both to the soup and carefully place the dumplings in between the vegetables. Cover and simmer for 20 minutes, or until the dumplings are fluffy and the potatoes are cooked. Check the seasoning.

5. While the dumplings are cooking, remove the beef from the freezer and using a sharp knife, slice into very thin slivers. Divide the beef between warmed soup bowls and ladle in the soup and dumplings. Serve at once.

NOTE: Make the consomme with three 200 g (7 oz) cans concentrated beef consommé and dilute according to the instructions on the label.

VARIATION

For cheese dumplings, omit the horseradish and add 25 g (1 oz) grated Gruyère or Cheddar cheese to the dumpling mixture. You may need a little extra water to bind the dough. Cook in the same way.

TECHNIQUE

Shape the dumpling dough into 12 small balls and carefully place between the vegetables in the soup.

CURRIED CARROT AND SPLIT PEA SOUP

There is undoubtedly something particularly warming about a curried lentil or split peas soup – the perfect remedy for a cold winter's night. Here split yellow peas are used to make a really thick and tasty soup. A tangy coriander and lime butter complements the soup perfectly, giving it a delicious finish. Alternatively you could omit the flavoured butter and simply sprinkle the soup with chopped coriander instead.

SERVES 4

50 g (2 oz) split yellow peas,
    soaked overnight in cold
    water
15 ml (1 tbsp) sunflower oil
1 small onion
1 garlic clove
225 g (8 oz) carrots
1 potato
1 red chilli
5 ml (1 tsp) grated fresh root
    ginger
7.5 ml (1½ tsp) hot curry
    paste
salt and pepper
**CORIANDER AND LIME
BUTTER**
50 g (2 oz) butter, softened
grated rind and juice of
    1 lime
7.5 ml (1½ tsp) chopped
    fresh coriander

PREPARATION TIME
35 minutes, plus overnight
soaking
COOKING TIME
1-1¼ hours
FREEZING
Suitable: Freeze separately,
wrapped in foil

260 CALS PER SERVING

1. Drain the split peas, rinse well and place in a large saucepan with 1.5 litres (2½ pints) cold water. Bring to the boil and boil steadily for 10 minutes. Reduce the heat, cover and simmer gently for 30 minutes.

2. Meanwhile, make the coriander and lime butter. In a bowl, cream the butter with the lime juice and rind, coriander and a little pepper, until evenly combined. Form into a log shape on a piece of greaseproof paper, overwrap in foil and chill in the refrigerator until required.

3. Peel and chop the onion, garlic, carrots and potato. Halve, deseed and chop the chilli. Heat the oil in a pan, add the onion, garlic, ginger and chilli and fry, stirring frequently, for 10 minutes until evenly browned. Stir in the curry paste, carrots and potato and fry for a further 5 minutes.

4. Add the curried vegetable mixture to the split peas. Return to the boil, cover and simmer for a further 35 minutes until the vegetables and peas are tender. Transfer to a blender or food processor and work until fairly smooth. Return to the pan, season with salt and pepper to taste and heat through.

5. Unwrap the butter and cut into thin slices. Pour the soup into warmed serving bowls and serve each portion topped with two slices of the flavoured butter.

VARIATION

Replace the split peas with red lentils, which do not require pre-soaking. Add 125 g (4 oz) red lentils to the fried curried vegetables, together with 1.2 litres (2 pints) vegetable stock (see page 5). Cook for 30 minutes until the vegetables and lentils are cooked.

TECHNIQUE

Transfer the soup to a food processor and blend until fairly smooth.

MUSHROOM AND ARTICHOKE SOUP WITH WALNUTS

Jerusalem artichokes can easily be confused as just another funny looking potato, but don't be fooled. These knobbly and often hairy root vegetables have a distinctive flavour of their own. The intense flavour of the mushroom stock combines beautifully with the artichokes, and the walnuts add texture to the finished soup.

SERVES 4

15 g (½ oz) dried ceps
150 ml (¼ pint) boiling
    water
1 small onion, peeled
450 g (1 lb) chestnut
    mushrooms
25 g (1 oz) butter
15 ml (1 tbsp) chopped fresh
    thyme
90 ml (3 fl oz) dry sherry
1.2 litres (2 pints) vegetable
    stock (see page 5)
450 g (1 lb) Jerusalem
    artichokes
1 garlic clove
30 ml (2 tbsp) walnut oil
salt and pepper
TO SERVE
25 g (1 oz) walnuts, chopped
    and toasted
extra walnut oil
thyme sprigs, to garnish

PREPARATION TIME
20 minutes, plus soaking
COOKING TIME
1½ hours
FREEZING Suitable

250 CALS PER SERVING

1. Put the dried ceps into a bowl, pour over the boiling water and let soak for 30 minutes. Drain, reserving the liquid.

2. Chop the onion and mushrooms. Melt the butter in a saucepan, add the onion and thyme and fry gently for 10 minutes until soft but not browned. Increase the heat, add the chestnut mushrooms and ceps and stir-fry for 2 minutes. Add the sherry and boil rapidly until well reduced.

3. Add the vegetable stock and reserved cep stock and bring to the boil. Cover and simmer gently for 20 minutes until the stock is rich tasting and the mushrooms have lost all their flavour.

4. Meanwhile, scrub the artichokes and cut away the knobbly bits. Peel, then dice the flesh. Peel and chop the garlic. Heat the oil in a large pan, add the artichokes and garlic and fry for 10 minutes, stirring, until evenly browned.

5. Strain the mushroom liquid through a fine sieve and add to the artichokes. Bring to the boil, cover and simmer for 35-40 minutes until the artichokes are cooked. Transfer to a blender or food processor and purée until very smooth.

6. Return the soup to the pan and heat gently for 5 minutes. Season with salt and pepper to taste and spoon into warmed soup bowls. Scatter the toasted nuts over the soup and drizzle with walnut oil. Serve at once, garnished with thyme.

NOTE: It is essential that the mushrooms impart their full flavour to the stock. Before straining the stock, check that they are quite tasteless.

VARIATION

Stir 150 ml (¼ pint) single cream into the puréed artichokes at the end of stage 5. Finish as above.

TECHNIQUE

Stir-fry the chestnut mushrooms and ceps over a high heat for 2 minutes.

SPINACH AND RICE SOUP WITH POACHED EGGS

This is my version of a classic Italian soup, where traditionally eggs and spinach are whisked together, then stirred into a hot stock to flavour and thicken it. I like to serve this soup topped with a soft poached egg, so that as you put your spoon into the soup the yolk breaks and mingles with the soup – it's delicious!

SERVES 4

1 onion
1 garlic clove
60 ml (4 tbsp) olive oil
5 ml (1 tsp) ground
   coriander
125 g (4 oz) Arborio rice
150 ml (¼ pint) dry white
   wine
1.2 litres (2 pints) chicken
   or vegetable stock (see
   pages 5-6)
4 small eggs (size 4)
350 g (12 oz) spinach leaves
60 ml (4 tbsp) chopped fresh
   parsley
salt and pepper
TO SERVE
cayenne pepper
freshly grated Parmesan
   cheese

PREPARATION TIME
20 minutes
COOKING TIME
40 minutes
FREEZING
Not suitable

390 CALS PER SERVING

1. Peel and chop the onion and garlic. Heat the oil in a large saucepan, add the onion, garlic and coriander and fry over a gentle heat for 10 minutes until softened but not coloured. Add the rice and stir-fry for 1-2 minutes until all the grains are glossy. Pour in the wine and boil rapidly for 3 minutes.

2. Add the stock, bring to the boil, cover and simmer over a low heat for 20 minutes until the rice is almost tender.

3. Heat a 5-7 cm (2-3 inch) depth of water in a small frying pan until it reaches simmering point. Very carefully break in the eggs to sit closely together. Return the water to a gentle simmer and cook until the egg whites are just set. Turn off the heat and cover the pan with a lid.

4. Roughly shred the spinach leaves and stir into the soup with the parsley. Cook for 2-3 minutes until the spinach has wilted and season with salt and pepper to taste. Spoon the soup into warmed bowls and carefully top each serving with a poached egg. Sprinkle with a little cayenne and plenty of freshly grated Parmesan. Serve at once.

VARIATION

Substitute the spinach with escarole (a bitter salad leaf). Omit the poached eggs and serve the soup topped with pesto (see page 42).

TECHNIQUE

Carefully break the eggs into a small frying pan of gently simmering water and cook until the egg whites are just set.

BUTTERNUT SQUASH SOUP WITH PARMESAN CROSTINI

Butternut is the club-shaped squash with a pale yellow skin and bright orange flesh. Its natural sweet buttery flavour needs little to enhance it and I like to cook it fairly simply. The creamy butternut flesh is ideal for puréeing, and both the sharpness of the Parmesan and the crisp bite of the crostini set it off beautifully – giving a really special soup for entertaining.

SERVES 4

1 large leek, trimmed
1 celery stick
1 garlic clove, peeled
1 small red chilli
350 g (12 oz) peeled and
    deseeded butternut
    squash (see note)
30 ml (2 tbsp) olive oil
15 ml (1 tbsp) chopped fresh
    sage
1 litre (1¾ pints) vegetable
    stock (see page 5)
pinch of cayenne pepper
salt and pepper
PARMESAN CROSTINI
4 thin slices day-old Ciabatta
    or French bread
2 garlic cloves, peeled
extra-virgin olive oil, for
    drizzling
25 g (1 oz) Parmesan cheese
salt and pepper

PREPARATION TIME
40 minutes
COOKING TIME
50 minutes
FREEZING
Suitable

185 CALS PER SERVING

1. Preheat the oven to 200°C (400°F) Mark 6. Slice the leek and celery; chop the garlic. Halve, deseed and chop the red chilli. Cut the squash into cubes.

2. Heat the oil in a saucepan, add the leek, celery and garlic and fry gently for 10 minutes. Add the sage, chilli and squash, and stir-fry for 5 minutes until the squash begins to colour.

3. Pour in the stock, add the cayenne and bring to the boil. Cover and simmer for 35 minutes, then transfer to a food processor and blend until smooth. Return to the pan, adjust the seasoning and heat through.

4. Meanwhile, make the crostini. Place the bread on a baking sheet and bake in the oven for 10 minutes. Rub each side with garlic, drizzle with a little oil and return to the oven for a further 10 minutes or until the bread is crisp and golden.

5. Spoon the soup into warmed bowls, and top with the crostini. Grate over the Parmesan and drizzle over a little more oil. Serve at once.

NOTE: To give this prepared weight of squash you will need about 450 g (1 lb).

VARIATION

For a curried version, add 30 ml (2 tbsp) hot curry paste to the onion, garlic and sage, omitting the chilli. Serve the soup topped with a spoonful of Greek-style yogurt and scattered with chopped fresh coriander.

TECHNIQUE

Rub the bread with garlic and drizzle with olive oil before baking.

CHILLED MELON AND GINGER SOUP

What could be more refreshing on a hot summer's day than a bowl of icy melon soup? The gingered cucumber relish sets off the flavour of the melon to perfection and adds an exotic element to the soup. For a special occasion serve the soup in the hollowed-out melon shells.

SERVES 4

4 small Charentais or
    Cantaloupe melons
4 spring onions, trimmed
60 ml (2 fl oz) ginger wine
15 ml (1 tbsp) chopped fresh
    dill
150 ml (¼ pint) crème
    fraîche or Greek yogurt
salt and pepper
lime juice, to taste
CUCUMBER RELISH
125 g (4 oz) cucumber
15 ml (1 tbsp) extra-virgin
    olive oil
5 ml (1 tsp) lime juice
15 ml (1 tbsp) chopped fresh
    dill
5 ml (1 tsp) chopped pre-
    served stem ginger, plus
    5 ml (1 tsp) syrup from jar
TO GARNISH
extra-virgin olive oil
dill sprigs

PREPARATION TIME
35 minutes, plus chilling
COOKING TIME
Nil
FREEZING
Suitable: Without cucumber
relish

285 CALS PER SERVING

1. Cut a very thin slice from the base of each melon so it will stand upright. Then cut another slice about 2.5 cm (1 inch) from the top. Place a sieve over a bowl and, holding the melon over the sieve to catch any juices, scoop out and discard the seeds. Scoop out and reserve the flesh along with the juices. Keep the melon shells for serving, if wished.

2. Place the melon flesh in a blender or food processor. Finely chop the spring onions and add to the melon with the ginger wine, dill and crème fraîche or yogurt. Purée until smooth, then blend in up to 300 ml (½ pint) of the reserved melon juice to give the required consistency. Season with salt and pepper, and add a little lime juice to taste. Chill in the refrigerator for 1 hour.

3. Meanwhile, make the cucumber relish. Peel and halve the cucumber, scoop out the seeds and very thinly slice the flesh. Sprinkle with salt and set aside for 30 minutes.

4. Wash the cucumber to remove the salt and pat dry on kitchen paper. Place in a bowl and stir in the remaining ingredients, seasoning with pepper to taste.

5. Divide the soup between the reserved melon shells or soup bowls and top each portion with a little of the cucumber relish. Drizzle over extra olive oil and serve garnished with dill.

VARIATION

Add 225 g (8 oz) cooked peeled prawns and process with the melon flesh, increasing the crème fraîche or yogurt to 300 ml (½ pint).

TECHNIQUE

Holding the melon over a sieve placed on a bowl to catch the juices, carefully scoop out and reserve the flesh.

CHILLED TOMATO SOUP WITH GUACAMOLE

Here Spain meets Mexico with a fairly classic gazpacho and a creamy guacamole – the traditional Mexican dip of puréed avocado, chillies, garlic and herbs. It is very important to use ripe flavourful tomatoes, so make this soup when tomatoes are at their best, most plentiful and consequently least expensive.

SERVES 6

900 g (2 lb) ripe tomatoes
175 g (6 oz) cucumber
6 large spring onions
I small red pepper
2 red chillies
50 g (2 oz) capers, drained
50 g (2 oz) pitted green
  olives, drained
50 g (2 oz) ground almonds
50 g (2 oz) fresh white
  breadcrumbs
30 ml (2 tbsp) chopped fresh
  coriander
5 ml (I tsp) sugar
45 ml (3 tbsp) balsamic
  vinegar
600 ml (I pint) cold vegetable
  stock (see page 5)
150 ml (¼ pint) tomato juice
125 ml (4 fl oz) extra-virgin
  olive oil
salt and pepper

GUACAMOLE

I small avocado
I red chilli
15 ml (I tbsp) Greek-style
  yogurt
I garlic clove, crushed
15 ml (I tbsp) lemon juice
15 ml (I tbsp) chopped fresh
  coriander
pinch of sugar

TO GARNISH

coriander sprigs
ice cubes, to serve

PREPARATION TIME 50 minutes, plus chilling
COOKING TIME Nil
FREEZING Not suitable

355 CALS PER SERVING

I. Immerse the tomatoes in a bowl of boiling water for 10 seconds, then remove with a slotted spoon and peel away the skins when cool enough to handle. Halve and deseed the tomatoes, roughly chop the flesh and place in a food processor. Peel, halve and deseed the cucumber, chop the flesh and add to the tomatoes.

2. Trim and chop the spring onions; halve, deseed and chop the red pepper and chillies. Add to the tomatoes and cucumber with the capers and olives. Work the mixture until very smooth, then gradually blend in the ground almonds, breadcrumbs, coriander, sugar and balsamic vinegar.

3. Transfer the mixture to a bowl and whisk in the stock, tomato juice and finally the olive oil. Season with salt and pepper to taste. Chill in the refrigerator for at least I hour.

4. Just before serving, make the guacamole. Halve, stone and peel the avocado. Halve, deseed and dice the chilli. Put the avocado and chilli in a blender or food processor with all the remaining ingredients and work to a purée. Season with salt and pepper to taste, adding a little more lemon juice if required.

5. Check the seasoning of the soup. Spoon into chilled serving bowls and top with the guacamole. Add a few ice cubes and serve, garnished with coriander.

VARIATION

For a green gazpacho, halve the quantity of tomatoes; use 2 green peppers instead of the red pepper; double the amount of cucumber.

TECHNIQUE

Whisk the stock, tomato juice and olive oil into the puréed soup.

TOMATO SALAD SOUP WITH BRUSCHETTA

The idea of a soup made from a salad may sound odd but it does make sense. The juices left from tomato salads are always so delicious that you inevitably dunk in some bread to mop them up. So why not make a tomato salad, leave it to allow the flavours to develop, then use as the basis of a really fresh tasting soup?

SERVES 4

700 g (1½ lb) ripe plum
 tomatoes
6 spring onions, trimmed
grated rind of ½ lemon
30 ml (2 tbsp) chopped fresh
 basil
125 ml (4 fl oz) extra-virgin
 olive oil
30 ml (2 tbsp) balsamic
 vinegar
1 garlic clove, crushed
pinch of sugar
60 ml (2 fl oz) chilled vodka
15 ml (1 tbsp)
 Worcestershire sauce
few drops of Tabasco
salt and pepper
150 ml (¼ pint) tomato
 juice
BRUSCHETTA TOPPING
8 thin slices French bread
1-2 garlic cloves, crushed
extra-virgin olive oil
TO GARNISH
basil leaves

PREPARATION TIME
15 minutes, plus marinating
COOKING TIME
4-5 minutes for bruschetta
FREEZING Not suitable

490 CALS PER SERVING

1. Thinly slice the tomatoes and place them in a large shallow dish. Finely chop the spring onions. Scatter the spring onions, lemon rind and basil over the tomatoes.

2. Blend together the olive oil, vinegar, garlic, sugar, vodka, Worcestershire sauce and Tabasco. Season with salt and pepper to taste and pour over the tomatoes. Cover and leave to marinate for 2 hours at room temperature.

3. Transfer the tomato salad to the blender or food processor. Add the tomato juice and purée until very smooth. Transfer to a bowl and chill in the refrigerator for 1 hour.

4. Just before serving, preheat the grill. Place the bread slices on the grill rack and toast lightly on both sides. Rub each one with garlic and drizzle with olive oil. Spoon the soup into serving bowls and float 2 slices of bruschetta on each portion. Garnish with basil and serve at once.

NOTE: Makes this soup during the summer months when tomatoes are at their best.

VARIATION

Serve the soup topped with a spoonful or two of olive paste.

TECHNIQUE

Pour the dressing evenly over the plate of sliced tomatoes, then cover and leave to marinate for 2 hours.

SPINACH AND PEA SOUP WITH LEMON

This vibrant green soup is quick and easy to make and I like the way the flavours work together especially with the addition of mint, a familiar partner of peas. Lemon juice, blended with extra-virgin olive oil, and shavings of salty Pecorino cheese, add a refreshing tang to the soup.

SERVES 4

1 onion
1 garlic clove
30 ml (2 tbsp) olive oil
2.5 ml (½ tsp) ground cumin
450 g (1 lb) spinach leaves
225 g (8 oz) shelled peas
(thawed if frozen)
30 ml (2 tbsp) chopped fresh
mint
900 ml (1½ pints) vegetable
or chicken stock (see
pages 5-6)
1.25 ml (¼ tsp) freshly
grated nutmeg
salt and pepper
TO GARNISH
60 ml (4 tbsp) extra-virgin
olive oil
30 ml (2 tbsp) lemon juice
fresh shavings of Pecorino
or Parmesan cheese

PREPARATION TIME
10 minutes
COOKING TIME
30 minutes
FREEZING
Suitable

300 CALS PER SERVING

1. Peel and chop the onion and garlic. Heat the oil in a saucepan, add the onion, garlic and cumin and fry gently for 10 minutes until lightly golden.

2. Wash and dry the spinach leaves and cut away the thick central stalks. Shred the leaves roughly and add to the pan with the peas, mint and stock.

3. Bring slowly to the boil, cover and simmer over a very gentle heat for 15 minutes.

4. Transfer the soup to a blender or food processor and blend until very smooth. Return to the pan and heat gently until the soup just reaches the boil. Add the nutmeg and season with salt and pepper to taste.

5. For the garnish, blend together the olive oil and lemon juice. Spoon the soup into warmed serving bowls and drizzle over the lemon oil. Scatter shavings of cheese on top and serve at once.

VARIATION

For a more substantial soup, add 225 g (8 oz) peeled and diced potatoes with the onion. Increase the quantity of stock to 1.2 litres (2 pints); add to the potatoes and onion and simmer for 15 minutes before stirring in the spinach, peas and mint. Finish as above.

TECHNIQUE

Cut away the thick central stalks from the spinach leaves before shredding them.

GRILLED PEPPER AND AUBERGINE SOUP

Peppers and aubergine become sweet as their flesh caramelises under the grill, giving this soup an intensity of flavour that is hard to surpass. The saffron cream garnish is similar to *rouille*.

SERVES 4-6

2 large red peppers
1 large aubergine
90 ml (3 fl oz) olive oil
1 large onion
2 garlic cloves
5 ml (1 tsp) grated lemon
  rind
15 ml (1 tbsp) chopped fresh
  thyme
5 ml (1 tsp) dried oregano
400 g (14 oz) can chopped
  tomatoes
900 ml (1½ pints) vegetable
  or chicken stock
1 bay leaf
30 ml (2 tbsp) chopped fresh
  basil
salt and pepper
SAFFRON CREAM
small pinch of saffron strands
1 egg yolk
1 garlic clove, crushed
2.5 ml (½ tsp) cayenne
  pepper
10 ml (2 tsp) lemon juice
150-175 ml (5-6 fl oz) olive oil

PREPARATION TIME
25 minutes
COOKING TIME
45-50 minutes
FREEZING
Suitable: Without saffron cream

390-300 CALS PER SERVING

1. Preheat the grill. Quarter, core and deseed the red peppers. Brush with a little olive oil and grill for 3-4 minutes on each side until charred and tender. Transfer to a plate, cover with a cloth and leave until cool enough to handle. Peel the peppers and roughly chop the flesh.

2. Thinly slice the aubergine lengthways. Brush with oil and grill for 4-5 minutes on each side until charred and tender. Leave until cool enough to handle, then chop roughly.

3. Peel and chop the onion and garlic. Heat the remaining oil in a large pan, add the onion, garlic, lemon rind, thyme and oregano and fry, stirring, for 10 minutes until browned. Add the peppers, aubergine, tomatoes, stock and bay leaf. Bring to the boil, cover and simmer for 20 minutes. Discard the bay leaf.

4. Meanwhile, make the saffron cream. Put the saffron in a small bowl, pour on 15 ml (1 tbsp) boiling water and leave to soak for 5 minutes. In a bowl, whisk the egg yolk with the garlic, cayenne, lemon juice and seasoning until pale and slightly thickened. Gradually whisk in the oil, until thick. Stir in the saffron liquid and seasoning to taste.

5. Transfer the soup to a blender or food processor. Add the basil and work until smooth. Return to the pan and heat through. Adjust the seasoning and pour into warmed soup bowls. Spoon a little saffron cream onto each portion, garnish with basil leaves and serve at once.

VARIATION

Replace the aubergine with 2 yellow peppers and grill as above. Divide all other ingredients in half and cook in separate pans, adding the red peppers to one and the yellow peppers to the other. Cook until tender and purée separately to give two different coloured pepper soups. Serve half and half in each bowl, swirling them attractively, and garnish with saffron cream.

TECHNIQUE

For the saffron cream, whisk in the oil a little at a time, beating well between each addition.

PASTA AND CHICK PEA SOUP WITH ROCKET PESTO

This soup similar to a minestrone with its selection of fresh green vegetables, but the pesto sauce is made with rocket, a peppery herb, rather than the more usual basil. The rocket gives a cleaner taste to the finished soup and adds a vivid splash of green.

SERVES 6

1 onion
2 garlic cloves
1 small leek, trimmed
4 ripe tomatoes
45 ml (3 tbsp) olive oil
15 ml (1 tbsp) chopped fresh
  rosemary
400 g (14 oz) can chick peas
1.2 litres (2 pints) vegetable
  stock (see page 5)
1 courgette, diced
125 g (4 oz) shelled peas
125 g (4 oz) French beans,
  halved
125 g (4 oz) shelled broad
  beans
50 g (2 oz) small pasta shells
30 ml (2 tbsp) chopped fresh
  parsley
salt and pepper
ROCKET PESTO
50 g (2 oz) rocket
1 garlic clove, peeled
15 ml (1 tbsp) capers, rinsed
  and drained
15 ml (1 tbsp) chopped fresh
  parsley
15 g (1/2 oz) pine nuts, toasted
15 g (1/2 oz) freshly grated
  Parmesan cheese
75 ml (5 tbsp) extra-virgin
  olive oil

PREPARATION TIME 25 minutes
COOKING TIME 1 hour
FREEZING Suitable: Without the pesto

370 CALS PER SERVING

1. Peel and chop the onion; peel and finely chop the garlic; slice the leek. Immerse the tomatoes in a bowl of boiling water for 10 seconds, then remove with a slotted spoon and peel away the skins. Chop the tomato flesh.

2. Heat the oil in a large saucepan, add the onion, garlic, leek and rosemary and fry gently for 10 minutes until softened but not coloured. Add the chick peas with their liquid, the stock and tomatoes. Bring to the boil, cover and simmer for 30 minutes.

3. Meanwhile make the rocket pesto. Wash and dry the rocket leaves and chop roughly. Place in a grinder or food processor and add the garlic, capers, parsley, pine nuts and Parmesan. Purée to form a fairly smooth paste, then stir in the oil and season with salt and pepper to taste.

4. Add the courgette, peas and beans to the soup. Return to the boil and simmer for a further 10 minutes. Add the pasta and parsley and cook for 6-8 minutes

until the pasta is *al dente* (tender but firm to the bite). Check the seasoning.

5. Spoon the soup into warmed bowls, add a spoonful of the rocket pesto to each one and serve at once.

VARIATION

Use borlotti beans instead of chick peas. Replace half the stock with an equal quantity of tomato juice. Substitute the peas with 125 g (4 oz) button mushrooms. Fry the mushrooms in 15 ml (1 tbsp) olive oil and add to the soup with the remaining green vegetables.

TECHNIQUE

For the pesto, process the rocket leaves with the garlic, capers, parsley, pine nuts and Parmesan to a fairly smooth paste.

GARLIC, BEAN AND TOMATO SOUP WITH PESTO

This is a soup for confirmed garlic lovers – a caramelised garlic broth forms the basis of the stock, and a garlic pesto sauce is served as a garnish. Caramelising raw garlic changes its character dramatically, giving it a far sweeter and milder flavour. Cooking it in this way also makes garlic more digestible.

SERVES 4

125 g (4 oz) dried borlotti
    beans, soaked overnight in
    cold water (see note)
1.2 litres (2 pints) vegetable
    stock (see page 5)
1 head of garlic
30 ml (2 tbsp) olive oil
450 g (1 lb) ripe tomatoes
15 ml (1 tbsp) lemon juice
salt and pepper
PESTO
1 garlic clove, chopped
2.5 ml ($\frac{1}{2}$ tsp) sea salt
25 g (1 oz) basil leaves
25 g (1 oz) pine nuts
125 ml (4 fl oz) extra-virgin
    olive oil
30 ml (2 tbsp) freshly grated
    Parmesan cheese

PREPARATION TIME
15 minutes, plus overnight
soaking
COOKING TIME
1 hour
FREEZING
Suitable: Without the pesto

530 CALS PER SERVING

1. Preheat the oven to 200°C (400°F), Mark 6. Drain and rinse the beans and place in a saucepan with the stock. Bring to the boil and boil rapidly for 10 minutes. Reduce the heat, cover and simmer for 40-45 minutes until the beans are tender.

2. Meanwhile, separate and peel the garlic cloves. Place them in a roasting tin, drizzle with the oil and bake near the top of the oven for 15 minutes. Meanwhile, roughly chop the tomatoes. Add to the garlic, stir to mix and bake for a further 10-15 minutes until the garlic is lightly browned and the tomatoes are soft. Set aside.

3. Transfer the cooked beans and their liquid to a blender or food processor, then add the tomato and garlic mixture, salt and pepper. Purée until fairly smooth, then return to the pan. Add the lemon juice and check the seasoning. Heat through for 5 minutes.

4. Meanwhile, make the pesto. Place the garlic, salt, basil and pine nuts in a food processor and blend until fairly smooth. Gradually blend in the oil. Stir in the cheese and salt and pepper to taste.

5. Ladle the soup into warmed bowls and top each serving with a spoonful of pesto.

NOTE: To save time, use a 400 g (14 oz) can borlotti or haricot beans rather than dried beans and reduce the stock to 900 ml (1$\frac{1}{2}$ pints). Rinse the beans before puréeing them with the stock and tomato mixture in step 3.

VARIATION

Add 225 g (8 oz) button mushrooms to the tomato and garlic mixture with an extra 15 ml (1 tbsp) olive oil. Bake as above, stir into the cooked beans and add 125 g (4 oz) each of peas, broad beans and diced broccoli. Cook until tender and serve topped with the pesto.

TECHNIQUE

Bake the garlic and tomatoes until soft and lightly browned.

NIÇOISE PLATTER

Serving a platter of tasty appetizers is such an enjoyable way to start a meal, enabling your guests to experience a range of different tastes and textures in one dish. This recipe is inspired by the flavours of Provence, and includes the rich olive paste – or tapenade as it's called in Nice – to spread onto grilled bread.

SERVES 8

400 g (14 oz) can cannellini
  beans, drained
grated rind and juice of 1
  lemon
2 garlic cloves, crushed
150 ml (¼ pint) extra-virgin
  olive oil
30 ml (2 tbsp) chopped fresh
  parsley
salt and pepper
225 g (8 oz) French beans
225 g (8 oz) radishes
4 eggs
8 large slices rustic-style
  bread (or 16 small slices)
OLIVE PASTE
125 g (4 oz) pitted black
  olives
1 garlic clove, crushed
2 anchovy fillets in oil,
  drained and chopped
30 ml (2 tbsp) chopped fresh
  parsley
60 ml (4 tbsp) extra-virgin
  olive oil
TO SERVE
lemon wedges
sea salt

PREPARATION TIME
40 minutes
COOKING TIME
15 minutes
FREEZING Not suitable

445 CALS PER SERVING

1. Start by making the olive paste. Using a pestle and mortar or a food processor, grind together the olives, garlic, anchovies, parsley and a little pepper until fairly smooth. Gradually blend in the oil. Season with salt and pepper to taste and set aside.

2. Rinse the cannellini beans, drain and place in a bowl. Stir in half the lemon juice and rind, half the garlic, 60 ml (4 tbsp) of the olive oil and the parsley. Season to taste and set aside.

3. Bring a large pan of water to the boil, add the French beans, return to the boil and simmer for 3 minutes. Drain and immediately refresh under cold running water; dry well. Toss the French beans with the remaining lemon juice, rind, garlic and a further 60 ml (4 tbsp) olive oil. Season to taste and set aside.

4. Wash the radishes and trim the leaves and root ends; cut in half if large. Toss with the remaining olive oil.

5. Bring a small pan of water to the boil, add the eggs, return to the boil and simmer gently for 7 minutes or longer if a firmer yolk is preferred. Drain and immediately plunge into iced water to cool. Peel and carefully cut in half.

6. Preheat the grill and toast the bread on both sides. Arrange all the ingredients on one large platter, with the olive paste in the centre. Serve garnished with lemon wedges, and pass around a pot of sea salt for the radishes.

VARIATION

If preferred use dried cannellini beans. Soak 200 g (7 oz) overnight in cold water; drain and rinse. Cook in a large pan with plenty of water to cover for 50-60 minutes until the beans are tender. Drain, refresh under cold running water and drain well. Continue as above.

TECHNIQUE

For the olive paste, grind together the olives, garlic, anchovies, parsley and a little pepper until fairly smooth.

CHICKEN, CASHEW AND NOODLE SALAD

Spicy fried strips of chicken, crisp green vegetables, herbs and toasted cashew nuts are tossed with noodles in a tangy soy dressing to create a fabulous explosion of taste and texture in the mouth. If time permits, allow the chicken to marinate for several hours for optimum flavour.

SERVES 4

350 g (12 oz) skinless
   chicken breast fillet
30 ml (2 tbsp) sunflower oil
5 ml (1 tsp) sesame oil
5 ml (1 tsp) ground coriander
1.25 ml (¼ tsp) chilli powder
pinch of Chinese five-spice
   powder
125 g (4 oz) dried egg
   noodles (½ packet)
50 g (2 oz) mangetout
50 g (2 oz) French beans,
   halved
15 ml (1 tbsp) chopped fresh
   mint
15 ml (1 tbsp) chopped fresh
   coriander
25 g (1 oz) cashew nuts,
   toasted

DRESSING

45 ml (3 tbsp) peanut or
   sunflower oil
10 ml (2 tsp) sesame oil
1 garlic clove, crushed
5 ml (1 tsp) grated fresh
   root ginger
2.5 ml (½ tsp) crushed dried
   red chilli flakes
15 ml (1 tbsp) dark soy sauce
15 ml (1 tbsp) lemon juice

TO GARNISH

coriander sprigs

PREPARATION TIME 25 minutes, plus marinating
COOKING TIME 4-5 minutes
FREEZING Not suitable

470 CALS PER SERVING

1. Very thinly slice the chicken breast, across the grain, then place in a shallow non-reactive dish. Combine 15 ml (1 tbsp) of the sunflower oil with the sesame oil, coriander, chilli powder and Chinese five-spice powder. Add to the chicken and stir until evenly coated. Cover and leave to marinate for at least 30 minutes.

2. Cook the noodles according to the packet instructions.

3. Heat the remaining sunflower oil in a large non-stick frying pan. When hot, add the marinated chicken pieces and stir-fry for 2 minutes until golden and crispy. Drain on kitchen paper.

4. Add the vegetables and herbs to the pan and stir-fry for 1 minute until tender. Add to the chicken pieces and keep warm.

5. To make the dressing, heat both oils in a small pan, add the garlic, ginger and chilli flakes and fry gently until softened but not coloured. Whisk in the soy sauce, lemon juice and 30 ml (2 tbsp) water. Bring to the boil and remove from the heat.

6. Drain the cooked noodles and immediately toss with the hot soy dressing and chicken and vegetable mixture. Sprinkle over the toasted cashews. Serve warm or cool, garnished with coriander.

VARIATION

Replace the chicken with the same weight of peeled, raw tiger prawns and add 10 ml (2 tsp) grated lime to the marinade. Stir-fry for 3-4 minutes until the prawns have turned pink. Use basil instead of mint and replace the lemon juice in the dressing with lime juice.

TECHNIQUE

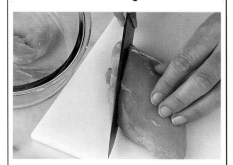

Slice the chicken breast very thinly across the grain into strips.

LEAF SALAD WITH GOAT'S CHEESE CROSTINI

This was inspired during a recent visit to Amsterdam where a friend ordered a similar toasted sandwich for a snack lunch. It was mouth-watering and quite delicious. . . and after several attempts here is a salad starter based on the idea.

SERVES 4

8 slices French bread

50 g (2 oz) French beans, trimmed

15 ml (1 tbsp) thyme-scented honey

15 ml (1 tbsp) extra-virgin olive oil

10 ml (2 tsp) chopped fresh thyme

125 g (4 oz) soft goat's cheese without rind

2 heads of chicory

50 g (2 oz) lamb's lettuce (or mâche)

25 g (1 oz) oak leaf lettuce

2 small peaches

DRESSING

60 ml (4 tbsp) walnut oil

5 ml (1 tsp) raspberry vinegar

5 ml (1 tsp) Dijon mustard

1.25 ml (¼ tsp) clear honey

salt and pepper

PREPARATION TIME
25 minutes
COOKING TIME
3-4 minutes
FREEZING
Not suitable

415 CALS PER SERVING

1. Preheat the grill and lightly toast the bread slices on both sides. Leave to cool.

2. Halve the French beans and blanch in a pan of lightly salted boiling water for 2 minutes. Drain, refresh under cold running water and dry well.

3. Meanwhile whisk together the honey, oil and thyme. Spread each piece of toast with goat's cheese, being careful to spread to the edges or they will burn. Drizzle over the honey and thyme mixture and return to the grill. Cook for 3-4 minutes until the cheese is bubbling and golden.

4. Slice the chicory and place in a bowl with the salad leaves. Halve, stone and slice the peaches and add to the salad with the French beans.

5. Put all the dressing ingredients in a screw-topped jar and shake vigorously to combine. Pour over the salad leaves, and divide between 4 serving plates. Sit 2 grilled toasts on each serving and serve at once.

NOTE: For convenience, use a bag of ready-prepared salad leaves in place of the lamb's lettuce, oak leaf lettuce and chicory.

TECHNIQUE

Drizzle the honey, oil and thyme mixture over the cheese toasts and grill until golden and bubbling.

PEPPERED SALMON ON A WATERCRESS AND POTATO SALAD

Fresh salmon fillets are encrusted with mixed crushed peppercorns, then very quickly seared over a high heat to cook just the outside, leaving the middle still rare. The salmon melts in the mouth and the salad provides a lovely contrast. Ask your fishmonger for thick fillets of salmon, cut from the head end of the fish.

SERVES 4

25 g (1 oz) mixed red,
    green, black and white
    peppercorns
4 skinless salmon fillets,
    each about 75 g (3 oz)
50 g (2 oz) watercress,
    stalks removed
350 g (12 oz) new potatoes
60 ml (2 fl oz) olive oil
MAYONNAISE
1 egg yolk
pinch of sugar
2.5 ml (½ tsp) Dijon
    mustard
1.25 ml (¼ tsp) sea salt
a little ground pepper
10 ml (2 tsp) lemon juice
150 ml (¼ pint) light olive
    oil
TO GARNISH
watercress sprigs

PREPARATION TIME
15 minutes
COOKING TIME
20 minutes
FREEZING
Not suitable

685 CALS PER SERVING

1. Using a pestle and mortar or a spice grinder, roughly grind the peppercorns. Transfer to a shallow dish.

2. Wash and dry the salmon fillets and, using a pair of tweezers, pull out any small bones that may remain. Press the salmon fillets well into the peppercorns to thoroughly coat the fish on all sides. Cover and set aside.

3. To make the mayonnaise, place the egg yolk, sugar, mustard, salt, pepper and lemon juice in a blender or small food processor and blend for 1 minute until pale. With the machine running, pour in the oil through the funnel in a steady stream, until the mayonnaise is thick and glossy, adding a little boiling water if too thick. Add the watercress and blend again until incorporated and the mayonnaise is a pale speckled green.

4. Halve or quarter the new potatoes if large. Cook in a large pan of lightly salted boiling water for 10-12 minutes until tender. Drain, then refresh briefly under cold running water to stop the cooking process. Drain and chop, then toss immediately with half the watercress mayonnaise until well coated.

5. Preheat a griddle or heavy-based frying pan, brush with oil and quickly sear the salmon by pressing down firmly on the hot surface for 1-2 minutes on each side to cook the salmon on the outside, but leave the centre rare. Arrange the potato salad on serving plates and top with the seared salmon fillets. Garnish with watercress and serve with the remaining mayonnaise.

NOTE: For convenience, use a good quality bought mayonnaise. Flavour 150 ml (¼ pint) with 10 ml (2 tsp) lemon juice and 2.5 ml (½ tsp) Dijon mustard. Blend with the watercress (as above).

TECHNIQUE

Sear the salmon fillets on both sides, pressing them down firmly to cook the outside but leave the centre rare.

SAVOURY HERB CUSTARDS WITH SMOKED SALMON

Individual savoury herb custards provide delicate bases for slices of smoked salmon and salmon caviar. The herbs are gently heated in the cream, then left to infuse before being strained off; this is sufficient to flavour the custards without overpowering them, while ensuring a smooth creamy texture.

SERVES 4

25 g (1 oz) fresh herbs, such
   as chives, parsley,
   tarragon, thyme, basil
350 ml (12 fl oz) double
   cream
3 eggs, lightly beaten
40 g (1½ oz) Gruyère
   cheese, finely grated
2.5 ml (½ tsp) celery salt
salt and pepper
125 g (4 oz) smoked salmon
25 g (1 oz) salmon caviar
15 ml (1 tbsp) chopped fresh
   chives
TO GARNISH
chives
salad leaves

PREPARATION TIME
15 minutes, plus infusing
COOKING TIME
25-30 minutes
FREEZING
Not suitable

555 CALS PER SERVING

1. Preheat the oven to 180°C (350°F) Mark 4. Lightly oil and base-line four 150 ml (¼ pint) timbale moulds or ramekin dishes. Wash and dry the herbs and bruise lightly with a rolling pin. Place in a small pan and add 300 ml (½ pint) of the cream. Bring slowly to the boil, remove from the heat and set aside to infuse for 30 minutes.

2. Strain the cream through a fine sieve into a bowl and blend in the eggs, Gruyère, celery salt and seasoning to taste. Pour into the moulds or ramekins and place in a roasting tin. Pour sufficient boiling water into the tin to come two thirds of the way up the sides of the dishes. Bake in the oven for 25 minutes until the custards are barely set in the centre. (They will set completely as they cool.)

3. Set aside for 30 minutes to cool, then remove the dishes from the roasting tin. Run a sharp knife around the edge of each custard to loosen it, then invert onto a serving plate.

4. Whip the remaining cream and top each herb custard with a slice of smoked salmon, a little whipped cream, some salmon caviar and chives. Serve at once, garnished with a sprig of chives and some salad leaves. Crisp French bread is an ideal accompaniment.

NOTE: These savoury custards are at their best served slightly warm, so don't bake them too far in advance.

VARIATION

Finely chop 25 g (1 oz) watercress or rocket leaves and mix with the cream, eggs, Gruyère, celery salt and pepper. Pour into the moulds and cook as above. Serve with a fresh tomato sauce (see page 54).

TECHNIQUE

Bruise the herbs with the rolling pin to release their flavour, before adding them to the cream.

RICOTTA QUENELLES WITH FRESH TOMATO SAUCE

This recipe was inspired during a recent trip to Rome. I was browsing through an Italian food magazine and a dish similar to this one caught my eye. In my version creamy herb-flavoured ricotta quenelles are served on a fresh-tasting tomato sauce. Toasted ciabatta or French bread makes a good accompaniment.

SERVES 4

350 g (12 oz) ricotta cheese
45 ml (3 tbsp) freshly grated
   Parmesan cheese
30 ml (2 tbsp) chopped fresh
   chives
15 ml (1 tbsp) chopped fresh
   chervil or parsley
5 ml (1 tsp) celery salt
1.25 ml ($\frac{1}{4}$ tsp) freshly
   grated nutmeg
salt and pepper
TOMATO SAUCE
900 g (2 lb) ripe tomatoes
125 ml (4 fl oz) olive oil
finely grated rind of 1 lemon
5 ml (1 tsp) salt
pinch of sugar
30 ml (2 tbsp) chopped fresh
   basil
15 ml (1 tbsp) balsamic
   vinegar
TO GARNISH
chives
chervil or parsley sprigs

PREPARATION TIME
35 minutes, plus chilling
COOKING TIME
45 minutes
FREEZING
Suitable: Tomato sauce only

505 CALS PER SERVING

1. Start by preparing the tomato sauce. Immerse the tomatoes in a bowl of boiling water for 10 seconds, then remove with a slotted spoon and peel away the skins. Halve, remove the seeds, then dice the tomato flesh.

2. Place the diced tomatoes, oil, lemon rind, salt, sugar and a little pepper in a small pan. Bring to the boil, cover and simmer over a low heat for 30 minutes. Remove the lid and simmer uncovered for a further 15 minutes to reduce and thicken. Leave to cool, then stir in the basil and vinegar and chill in the refrigerator.

3. To make the quenelles, place the ricotta in a bowl and beat or whisk for several minutes until light and fluffy. Fold in the grated Parmesan, herbs, celery salt, nutmeg and seasoning to taste. Chill in the refrigerator for at least 1 hour.

4. Using 2 dessertspoons, form the chilled ricotta mixture into 12 quenelles or 'egg shapes', by passing the mixture between the spoons.

5. Spoon the tomato sauce onto serving plates and arrange the ricotta quenelles on top. Garnish with chives and chervil or parsley. Serve accompanied by toasted ciabatta or French bread.

VARIATION

When fresh tomatoes are not at their best use canned ones instead: you will need two 400 g (14 oz) cans chopped tomatoes. Prepare the tomato sauce as above, omitting the final uncovered simmering stage.

TECHNIQUE

Shape the ricotta mixture into quenelles using 2 dessertspoons. Pass each heaped spoonful of the mixture between the spoons to form an oval or 'egg shape'.

PORK AND LIVER PÂTÉ

Owing to an inquisitive nature I'm always intrigued to discover what lies in wait under butter sealed pâté! Here we have a rich savoury pork and chicken liver mixture flavoured with Calvados and ground mixed spice. The accompanying caramelised onions with rosemary and balsamic vinegar set the pâté off perfectly. Serve with Melba toast or wholemeal bread. The pâté will keep in the refrigerator for up to 3 days.

SERVES 4

50 g (2 oz) piece pancetta or
    smoked bacon
125 g (4 oz) chicken livers
1 small onion
125 g (4 oz) unsalted butter
1 garlic clove, crushed
5 ml (1 tsp) chopped fresh
    thyme
60 ml (2 fl oz) Calvados or
    brandy
2.5 ml (½ tsp) ground mixed
    spice
pinch of cayenne pepper
25 g (1 oz) fresh white
    breadcrumbs
salt and pepper
225 g (8 oz) cooked pork,
    diced
4-6 bay leaves
ROSEMARY ONIONS
450 g (1 lb) baby onions
50 g (2 oz) butter
pinch of sugar
15-30 ml (1-2 tbsp) chopped
    fresh rosemary
45 ml (3 tbsp) balsamic
    vinegar

PREPARATION TIME
30 minutes
COOKING TIME
30-35 minutes
FREEZING
Suitable: Pâté only

560 CALS PER SERVING

1. Dice the pancetta or bacon. Trim and dice the chicken livers. Peel and finely grate the onion.

2. Heat a heavy-based frying pan, add the pancetta or bacon and stir-fry over a high heat until it is browned and has released some fat. Add 25 g (1 oz) of the unsalted butter and fry the onion and garlic for 5 minutes until golden. Add the chicken livers and thyme and stir-fry for 2 minutes until the livers are browned.

3. Lower the heat and stir in the Calvados or brandy, mixed spice and cayenne. Cover the pan and simmer for 5 minutes. Remove from the heat and leave to cool.

4. Transfer the mixture to a food processor, add the breadcrumbs and seasoning and blend until fairly smooth. Add the pork, pulse briefly and spoon into 1 large or 4 small pâté dishes. Smooth the surface.

5. Melt the remaining butter, cool slightly, then pour over the pâté. Leave to cool until the butter is almost set, then press in the bay leaves. Chill for several hours or overnight.

6. Meanwhile prepare the rosemary onions. Peel and halve the baby onions. Melt the butter in a frying pan, add the onions and cook over a medium heat for 15 minutes until golden and caramelised. Stir in the sugar, a little salt and rosemary to taste. Continue to fry for a further 3 minutes. Stir in the vinegar and 30 ml (2 tbsp) water. Bring to the boil and remove from the heat. Leave until cold, then season with salt and pepper to taste.

7. Serve the pâté with the onions and Melba toast or wholemeal bread.

VARIATION

Replace the pork with cooked chicken breast fillet. Flavour the onions with thyme rather than rosemary.

TECHNIQUE

Cook the baby onions until golden and caramelised, then stir in the sugar, salt and chopped rosemary.

GRILLED PEPPERS WITH MOZZARELLA

This dish is based on a classic Italian pepper dish from Piedmont – known as Piedmontese peppers. Here the halved peppers are grilled until their skins char and the flesh becomes sweet and tender. Once cooled the peppers are stuffed with olives, anchovies, capers and small balls of mozzarella – called bocconcini. Serve the peppers with plenty of Italian bread to mop up the delicious juices.

SERVES 4-8

4 large red peppers
olive oil, for drizzling
2 garlic cloves, crushed
8 balls bocconcini
  mozzarella (see note)
50 g (2 oz) can anchovies in
  oil, drained and roughly
  chopped
50 g (2 oz) black olives
15 g (½ oz) capers, drained
  and rinsed
15 ml (1 tbsp) chopped fresh
  basil
15 ml (1 tbsp) chopped fresh
  parsley
BALSAMIC DRESSING
15 ml (1 tbsp) balsamic
  vinegar
150 ml (¼ pint) extra-virgin
  olive oil
salt and pepper
TO GARNISH
basil sprigs

PREPARATION TIME
15 minutes
COOKING TIME
25-30 minutes, plus cooling
FREEZING
Not suitable

650-325 CALS PER SERVING

1. Preheat the grill. Cut each pepper in half lengthways through the stalk and scoop out the seeds. Place cut-side down on the grill pan, brush with oil and grill for 15 minutes until the skins are charred. Turn the peppers over, sprinkle a little garlic into each half and drizzle over a little more oil. Grill for a further 10-15 minutes until the peppers are very tender. Transfer to a large platter and leave to cool to room temperature.

2. Just before serving mix together the mozzarella balls, anchovies, olives, capers and herbs. For the dressing, blend the balsamic vinegar with the olive oil and season with salt and pepper to taste. Stir a little of the dressing into the mozzarella mixture and toss to coat lightly.

3. Spoon the filling into the cool pepper halves, arrange on serving plates and drizzle the remaining dressing over the peppers. Garnish with basil and serve at once, with plenty of crusty bread.

NOTE: If bocconcini mozzarella balls are unobtainable, simply use a 150 g (5 oz) mozzarella cheese, cut into small cubes.

VARIATION

Peel, halve and deseed 8 plum tomatoes. Sit 2 tomato halves in each pepper half, after turning them under the grill. Cook until tender. Immediately spoon in the olives, anchovies, capers and half the dressing. Top each pepper with slices of mozzarella and return to the grill for 5 minutes until golden.

TECHNIQUE

Grill the pepper halves cut-side down on the grill pan until the skins are charred, then turn cut-side up and sprinkle with garlic and olive oil.

SKEWERED SCALLOPS WITH LENTIL SALAD

Scallops with their vibrant orange corals are the jewels of the sea. Make sure you buy really fresh ones from a good fishmonger, as the delicate sweet flavour of the scallops is vital to the success of this dish. If using bamboo skewers, soak in cold water for 30 minutes prior to use, to prevent them from burning.

SERVES 4

12 large fresh scallops
15 ml (1 tbsp) olive oil, for
  brushing
MARINADE
60 ml (4 tbsp) olive oil
60 ml (4 tbsp) dry white wine
1 garlic clove, peeled and
  chopped
15 ml (1 tbsp) chopped fresh
  rosemary
15 ml (1 tbsp) chopped fresh
  chervil
2.5 ml ($\frac{1}{2}$ tsp) coriander
  seeds, crushed
2.5 ml ($\frac{1}{2}$ tsp) fennel seeds,
  crushed
SALAD
125 g (4 oz) Puy lentils
4 shallots
1 garlic clove
1 small red chilli
50 g (2 oz) fennel, chopped
grated rind and juice of 1
  lemon
30 ml (2 tbsp) olive oil
90 ml (3 fl oz) fish or vegetable stock (see pages 5-6)
125 g (4 oz) spinach leaves
salt and pepper
TO SERVE
herb sprigs, to garnish
lemon wedges

PREPARATION TIME 15 minutes, plus
marinating
COOKING TIME 50 minutes
FREEZING Not suitable

430 CALS PER SERVING

1. Shell the scallops if necessary, by prising open the shells with a strong knife and severing the muscle, then carefully loosening the scallop. Trim off the beard-like fringe and cut away the tough grey muscle at one side. Rinse well.

2. Combine all the marinade ingredients in a shallow dish. Add the scallops, toss well, cover and leave to marinate for at least 4 hours.

3. For the salad, place the lentils in a saucepan with plenty of cold water. Bring to the boil, cover and simmer for 35-40 minutes until tender. Drain well.

4. Remove the scallops from their marinade and dry well on kitchen paper. Thread them onto 4 skewers. Strain and reserve the marinade.

5. Peel and chop the shallots and garlic. Halve, deseed and chop the chilli. Chop the fennel. Heat the oil in a frying pan and fry the shallots, garlic, chilli, fennel and lemon rind for 5 minutes until lightly golden. Stir in the cooked lentils with

the stock, reserved marinade and lemon juice. Cover and simmer for 5 minutes. Shred the spinach, add to the pan and cook until just wilted. Season with salt and pepper and keep warm.

6. Preheat the grill. Place the skewered scallops on a foil-lined grill pan and brush with the oil. Grill as close to the heat as possible, turning and basting frequently, for 3-4 minutes, until golden and cooked through. Alternatively cook the scallops on an oiled hot griddle or heavy-based frying pan for 1-1$\frac{1}{2}$ minutes each side.

7. Spoon the lentil salad onto warmed serving plates and top each one with a skewer of scallops. Garnish with herbs and serve at once, with lemon wedges.

TECHNIQUE

Thread 3 scallops onto each of 4 skewers, passing the skewers through the corals and white meat to hold them together.

POTATO PANCAKES WITH MUSTARD CHICKEN LIVERS

As you eat this tasty starter, the light fluffy potato pancakes melt in the mouth along with the just cooked chicken livers. The whole dish is perfectly rounded off by a mustard crème fraîche sauce. Always check that your guests are happy to eat offal before choosing this recipe.

SERVES 4

PANCAKES
225 g (8 oz) floury potatoes
I small egg (size 5), or ½
size 2 egg
30 ml (2 tbsp) milk
20 ml (1½ tbsp) self-raising
flour
5 ml (I tsp) chopped fresh
thyme
1.25 ml (¼ tsp) salt
I egg white
a little vegetable oil, for
frying
SAUCE
50 g (2 oz) crème fraîche
15 ml (I tbsp) wholegrain
mustard
7.5 ml (1½ tsp) lemon juice
15 ml (I tbsp) chopped fresh
chives
CHICKEN LIVERS
2 shallots
25 g (I oz) butter
225 g (8 oz) chicken livers,
thawed if frozen
salt and pepper
TO SERVE
50 g (2 oz) lamb's lettuce
extra-virgin olive oil
lemon juice, to taste
chives and lemon wedges, to
garnish

PREPARATION TIME 20 minutes
COOKING TIME 25-30 minutes
FREEZING Suitable: Pancakes only. Thaw at room temperature. Reheat in a moderate oven for 5 minutes.

335 CALS PER SERVING

1. Peel the potatoes and cut into even-sized pieces. Cook in lightly salted boiling water for 12-15 minutes until tender. Drain well and mash until very smooth. Allow to cool slightly, then whisk in the egg, milk, flour, thyme and salt to form a thick smooth batter.

2. Meanwhile, make the sauce. In a bowl, mix together the crème fraîche, mustard, lemon juice and chives. Set aside to allow the flavours to develop.

3. Whisk the egg white and carefully fold into the pancake batter.

4. Preheat the oven to its lowest setting. Heat a very thin layer of oil in a frying pan. Pour in 2 large spoonfuls of the batter to form small pancakes and cook for 1-2 minutes until golden. Flip the pancakes over and cook the other side until golden. Drain on kitchen paper and keep warm in the oven. Repeat with the remaining mixture to make 8 pancakes in total.

5. Peel and slice the shallots. Melt the butter in a small frying pan, add the shallots and fry gently for 5 minutes until just golden. Increase the heat, add the chicken livers and stir-fry for 3-4 minutes until the livers are well browned on the outside, but still a little pink in the centre. Season with salt and pepper to taste.

6. Toss the lamb's lettuce with a little oil and lemon juice. Arrange the potato pancakes on warmed serving plates. Sit the livers on top, scraping over any pan juices, and add a spoonful of the mustard sauce. Garnish with the salad, chives and lemon wedges.

TECHNIQUE

Add 2 large spoonfuls of batter to the hot oil and cook for 1-2 minutes until golden. Turn and cook the other side of the pancakes.

DIVINE SPARE RIBS

In this recipe the ribs are first simmered to tenderise the meat before being roasted with a tangy Chinese-style glaze – resulting in succulent, tender ribs. Remember to give each guest a finger bowl of warm water – eating ribs can be a messy business!

SERVES 4

900 g (2 lb) pork spare ribs
30 ml (2 tbsp) malt vinegar
30 ml (2 tbsp) sesame oil
90 ml (3 fl oz) rice or wine
vinegar
60 ml (2 fl oz) dark soy
sauce
10 ml (2 tsp) grated fresh
root ginger
1 garlic clove, crushed
grated rind of 1 lime
60 ml (4 tbsp) soft brown
sugar
2.5 ml (½ tsp) Chinese five-
spice powder
90 ml (3 fl oz) water
TO GARNISH
coriander sprigs
lime wedges

PREPARATION TIME
15 minutes
COOKING TIME
1½ hours
FREEZING
Suitable: For up to 1 month.
Thaw at room temperature;
reheat in a covered dish in a
moderate oven for 20 minutes.

280 CALS PER SERVING

1. Wash and dry the spare ribs and place in a saucepan. Cover with plenty of cold water and add the malt vinegar. Bring to the boil and simmer for 20 minutes, skimming the surface from time to time to remove the scum.

2. Preheat the oven to 220°C (425°F) Mark 7. Meanwhile, place all the remaining ingredients in a small pan, bring to the boil and simmer for 5 minutes until reduced and thickened slightly.

3. Drain the ribs and transfer to a roasting dish that will hold the ribs in a single layer. Pour over the soy mixture and toss the ribs to coat evenly.

4. Cover loosely with foil and roast in the oven for 30 minutes. Remove the foil and cook for a further 30 minutes, turning and basting the ribs every 5 minutes. Leave to cool slightly for about 10 minutes before serving.

5. Garnish with coriander and lime wedges, and provide finger bowls and plenty of napkins.

VARIATION

Barbecued chicken wings make a tasty alternative to the pork ribs. Omit the par-boiling stage. Roast as above, coated with the glaze, for the same time or until glazed and tender.

TECHNIQUE

Turn the ribs and baste with the glaze every 5 minutes during the second half of roasting.

ASPARAGUS, ROCKET AND PARMA HAM BRUSCHETTA

A classic Italian bruschetta is a simple affair of grilled bread, rubbed all over with garlic and drizzled generously with fruity extra-virgin olive oil. However you can, of course, be more creative and top the toasts with all sorts of grand combinations. The flavours used here – asparagus, rocket and Parma ham – are frequent partners, providing a fabulous topping and a sumptuous starter.

SERVES 4

225 g (8 oz) asparagus
50 ml (2 fl oz) extra-virgin
    olive oil
4 large thick slices of rustic
    bread
1 garlic clove, halved
50 g (2 oz) rocket
4 slices of Parma ham
DRESSING
25 ml (1 fl oz) extra-virgin
    olive oil
5 ml (1 tsp) lemon juice
1.25 ml ($\frac{1}{4}$ tsp) thin honey
salt and pepper
TO SERVE
shavings of Parmesan
    cheese

PREPARATION TIME
10 minutes
COOKING TIME
8-10 minutes
FREEZING
Not suitable

350 CALS PER SERVING

1. Preheat the oven to its lowest setting and preheat the grill. Trim the woody ends of the asparagus and peel the lower ends of the stalks to remove any tough stringy parts if necessary. Brush with a little of the oil and grill for 4-5 minutes, turning frequently, until the asparagus spears are charred and tender. Transfer to a small warmed dish and keep warm in the oven.

2. Toast the bread lightly on both sides and rub all over with garlic. Drizzle liberally with olive oil and keep warm in the oven with the asparagus.

3. Place the rocket in a small bowl. To make the dressing, put the oil in a screw-topped jar with the lemon juice, honey and salt and pepper; shake vigorously to combine. Pour the dressing over the rocket and toss to coat all the leaves.

4. Remove the asparagus and bread from the oven. Arrange the bruschetta on serving plates and top each with a handful of the dressed rocket leaves, a few asparagus spears and a slice of Parma ham. Top with shavings of Parmesan and serve at once, drizzled with a little extra olive oil if wished.

VARIATION

Spread each slice of bruschetta with rocket pesto (see page 40), then top with some frisée (curly endive), the asparagus, Parma ham and Parmesan.

TECHNIQUE

Pour the dressing over the rocket leaves and toss lightly until the leaves are evenly coated.

ROASTED MUSHROOMS WITH LEMON AND GARLIC OIL

As a child I was fortunate enough to live on a farm, where mushrooms grew in abundance. I can remember discovering the most enormous field mushrooms with my father in the early autumn. . .this recipe takes me back to those days. You will need to prepare the oil infusion 3 days in advance.

SERVES 4

2 garlic cloves
2.5 ml (½ tsp) sea salt
finely pared rind of 1 lemon
150 ml (¼ pint) olive oil
8 large flat field mushrooms
　　each about 12 cm
　　(5 inches) across
30 ml (2 tbsp) chopped fresh
　　parsley
salt and pepper
lemon wedges, to serve

PREPARATION TIME
5 minutes, plus 3 days infusing
COOKING TIME
20-25 minutes
FREEZING
Not suitable

350 CALS PER SERVING

1. Crush the garlic and salt together with a pestle and mortar or on a chopping board and place in a jar. Add the lemon rind and pour in the oil. Shake well to ensure that the garlic and lemon are covered by the oil and seal the jar. Refrigerate for 3 days.

2. When ready to prepare the mushrooms, preheat the oven to 220°C (425°F) Mark 7. Place the mushrooms, stalk-side up, in a shallow roasting tin in which they fit closely together.

3. Drizzle two thirds of the oil liberally over the mushrooms and bake in the oven for 15 minutes. Turn the mushrooms over and baste with more oil. Bake for a further 5-10 minutes until the mushrooms are tender and browned, basting occasionally.

4. Arrange the mushrooms on a large warmed serving plate and scatter over the chopped parsley. Season with salt and pepper. Serve at once, with lemon wedges and accompanied by any remaining infused oil.

VARIATION

To barbecue the mushrooms, place, stalk-side up, on a doubled piece of foil, pour over the infused oil and seal the foil. Cook over the coals for 20 minutes and serve straight from the parcels.

TECHNIQUE

Baste the mushrooms with oil during roasting to ensure that they will be moist and tender.

QUICK MOZZARELLA AND SALAMI PIZZAS

This is an ideal starter for an informal supper, as it is quick and easy to prepare and cook – and tastes absolutely delicious. The recipe was given to me by a friend, who I work with regularly. He serves it as a supper dish, allowing one 1 whole roll per person, but I prefer it as a starter.

SERVES 4

2 ciabatta rolls
60 ml (2 fl oz) olive oil
    (optional)
30 ml (2 tbsp) sun-dried
    tomato paste
1 large ripe beefsteak
    tomato
12 large basil leaves
50 g (2 oz) salami
150 g (5 oz) mozzarella
    cheese, thinly sliced
5 ml (1 tsp) dried oregano
extra-virgin olive oil, for
    drizzling
TO GARNISH
basil sprigs

PREPARATION TIME
20 minutes
COOKING TIME
15-20 minutes
FREEZING
Not suitable

435 CALS PER SERVING

1. Preheat the oven to 220°C (425°F) Mark 7. Slice each roll in half horizontally. Heat the oil in a large frying pan and fry the halved rolls for 2-3 minutes until crisp and golden on both sides. Drain on kitchen paper. (Alternatively lightly toast the rolls on both sides.)

2. Spread the cut sides of the rolls with a little sun-dried tomato paste. Cut the beef tomato into 4 thick slices and place a slice on each roll half. Top each one with 3 basil leaves, some salami and mozzarella slices.

3. Transfer the pizzas to a baking sheet and scatter over the oregano. Drizzle with a little olive oil and bake near the top of the oven for 10-15 minutes until the cheese is bubbling and golden. Serve at once, garnished with a little basil.

VARIATION

Vary the toppings for these pizzas as you wish. Try spreading the fried or toasted halved rolls with olive paste (see page 44) and top the tomato slices with some chopped anchovies and capers. Bake as above.

TECHNIQUE

Top the fried or toasted rolls with sun-dried tomato paste, tomato, basil, salami and mozzarella. Sprinkle oregano over the top.

VEGETABLE AND PRAWN ROSTI WITH MANGO SALSA

The credit for this recipe must go to the person who inspired its origination. I was making some little vegetable rostis while working with Graham Kirk, a food photographer, and he suggested the addition of prawns. Well, Graham, here they are: I hope you approve!

SERVES 4

350 g (12 oz) mixed root
    vegetables, such as
    potato, celeriac, carrot,
    parsnip
½ small onion, peeled
125 g (4 oz) cooked peeled
    prawns
15 g (½ oz) plain flour
1 egg, lightly beaten
salt and pepper
vegetable oil, for frying
MANGO SALSA
½ small mango, about 175 g
    (6 oz) peeled weight
2 ripe tomatoes
1 red chilli
4 spring onions, trimmed
15 ml (1 tbsp) chopped fresh
    coriander
15 ml (1 tbsp) chopped fresh
    chives
15 ml (1 tbsp) lemon juice
15 ml (1 tbsp) light soy
    sauce
15 ml (1 tbsp) extra-virgin
    olive oil

PREPARATION TIME
40 minutes, plus infusing
COOKING TIME
15 minutes
FREEZING Not suitable

275 CALS PER SERVING

1. Start by making the salsa. Chop the mango flesh finely. Immerse the tomatoes in boiling water for 10 seconds, then remove and peel away the skins. Halve, deseed and dice the tomato flesh. Halve, deseed and dice the chilli. Finely chop the spring onions. Mix all the salsa ingredients together in a bowl. Season with salt and pepper to taste and set aside for 30 minutes to allow the flavours to infuse.

2. Using either a food processor with a grater attachment or the finer side of a box grater, finely grate all the root vegetables. Squeeze out the excess liquid and combine the vegetables in a large bowl. Grate the onion and add to the bowl. Roughly chop the prawns and add to the vegetables with the flour, egg and seasoning. Mix until evenly combined.

3. Divide the vegetable mixture into 4 equal portions and press each portion into a greased 10 cm (4 inch) plain pastry cutter. Alternatively make 8 smaller rostis forming them in 5 cm (2 inch) cutters.

4. Heat a shallow layer of oil in a large non-stick frying pan. Transfer the rostis, still in the cutters, to the pan. As soon as the mixture sizzles, remove the cutters and fry, pressing down with a spatula, for 6-8 minutes on each side, until crisp and golden. Drain on kitchen paper and serve hot, with the mango salsa.

VARIATION

Replace the prawns with 1 large, un-ripe pear; peeled, cored and grated. Shape the mixture into 8 large thin cakes and fry for 2-3 minutes on each side until crisp and golden. Top the cooked rostis with smoked salmon and crème fraîche to serve.

TECHNIQUE

Shape the rostis in greased 10 cm (4 inch) plain pastry cutters, then carefully transfer to the frying pan. Remove the cutters when the mixture sizzles.

HERB GNOCCHI WITH GRILLED TOMATO SAUCE

Gnocchi are Italian potato dumplings, a rustic dish, but non the less, totally delicious. As they are filling you only need to serve a small portion as a starter. Here they are served with a grilled tomto sauce, which has a lovely smoky flavour. Use a combination of red cherry and yellow cherry or pear tomatoes if possible, as this looks really stunning.

SERVES 4

450 g (I lb) floury potatoes
I egg
5 ml (I tsp) salt
15 ml (I tbsp) finely
  chopped fresh rosemary
60-75 g (2½-3 oz) plain flour
SAUCE
450 g (I lb) mixed red and
  yellow cherry tomatoes
2 garlic cloves, peeled and
  sliced
5 ml (I tsp) grated lemon rind
15 ml (I tbsp) chopped fresh
  thyme
15 ml (I tbsp) chopped fresh
  basil
30 ml (2 tbsp) olive oil
salt and pepper
pinch of sugar
TO SERVE
extra-virgin olive oil
freshly grated Parmesan
  cheese
rosemary sprigs, to garnish

PREPARATION TIME
25 minutes
COOKING TIME
25-30 minutes
FREEZING Not suitable

245 CALS PER SERVING

1. Preheat the oven to its lowest setting. Cook the potatoes in lightly salted boiling water for 15-20 minutes until cooked; drain well and return to the pan. Set over a gentle heat to dry the potatoes out and leave to cool slightly.

2. Bring a large pan of water to a steady simmer. Mash the potatoes smoothly, then work in the egg, salt, rosemary and enough flour to form a soft dough. Add a little more flour if the mixture is too sticky. Transfer to a piping bag fitted with a large plain nozzle.

3. Meanwhile make the sauce. Preheat the grill. Halve the tomatoes and place in a flameproof dish. Add the garlic, lemon rind, herbs, oil and seasoning and toss together. Sprinkle over the sugar and grill as close to the heat as possible for 10 minutes until the tomatoes are charred and tender.

4. While the tomatoes are grilling cook the gnocchi, in batches. Pipe about six 5 cm (2 inch) lengths directly into the boiling water, using a sharp knife to cut them off at the nozzle. Cook for 3-4 minutes until the gnocchi float to the surface.

5. Remove with a slotted spoon, drain on kitchen paper and transfer to a large warmed bowl. Toss with a little olive oil and keep warm in the oven while cooking the remaining potato mixture.

6. Toss the cooked gnocchi with the grilled tomato sauce. Serve immediately, dusted with a little freshly grated Parmesan and garnished with rosemary.

VARIATION

Transfer the cooked gnocchi to 4 individual gratin dishes, spoon over the tomato sauce and top with slices of mozzarella and a little grated Parmesan. Grill for 3-4 minutes. Serve at once.

TECHNIQUE

Cook the gnocchi in batches. Pipe 5 cm (2 inch) lengths directly into the boiling water from the piping bag.

BABY ONION AND FRESH PEA RISOTTO

Sweet, tender caramelised baby onions add a rich depth of flavour to this risotto. The peas add colour and texture as you bite into them – for this it really is best to use fresh peas in season. Frozen ones can be used when fresh peas are unavailable, but stir them into the risotto at the end, just to heat through.

SERVES 4

225 g (8 oz) baby onions
50 g (2 oz) butter
30 ml (2 tbsp) olive oil
4 garlic cloves, peeled
30 ml (2 tbsp) chopped fresh
**   sage**
10 ml (2 tsp) soft brown
**   sugar**
5 ml (1 tsp) sea salt
225 g (8 oz) arborio or
**   risotto rice**
150 ml (¼ pint) red wine
60 ml (2 fl oz) ruby port
**   (optional)**
900 ml-1.2 litres (1½-2
**   pints) vegetable stock**
125 g (4 oz) shelled peas
**   (see note)**
15-30 ml (1-2 tbsp) olive
**   paste (see page 44)**
25 g (1 oz) freshly grated
**   Parmesan cheese**
TO GARNISH
sage sprigs

PREPARATION TIME
30 minutes
COOKING TIME 35 minutes,
plus 5 minutes standing
FREEZING Not suitable

495 CALS PER SERVING

1. Put the baby onions in a saucepan of cold water. Bring to the boil and simmer for 30 seconds, then drain and refresh under cold water. Peel away the skins and halve the onions if large.

2. Melt half the butter with the oil in a frying pan. Add the onions and garlic cloves and fry over a medium heat for 15 minutes, stirring occasionally, until caramelised. Stir in the sage, sugar and salt and fry for a further 10 minutes.

3. Meanwhile, melt the remaining butter in a heavy-based, non-stick frying pan. Add the rice and stir-fry for 1-2 minutes until all the grains are glossy. Add the wine, and port if using, and boil rapidly until almost totally reduced.

4. Heat the stock in a small pan and keep it at a very gentle simmer. Gradually add the simmering stock to the rice, a ladleful at a time, stirring the rice constantly and making sure each addition is absorbed before adding the next. Continue for about 20 minutes, until most of the stock has been added and the rice is almost cooked.

5. Add the onion mixture to the rice with the remaining stock and the peas and continue to cook, stirring, until the liquid is absorbed and the rice is *al dente* (cooked but firm to the bite). Remove the pan from the heat and stir in the olive paste and two thirds of the Parmesan. Season, cover with foil and allow the risotto to stand for 5 minutes.

6. Serve topped with the remaining Parmesan and garnished with sage.

NOTE: For this quantity you will need 300 g (10 oz) fresh peas in the pod.

VARIATION

Replace the olive paste with sun-dried tomato paste. Like olive paste, this is available in jars or can easily be made at home. Purée 50 g (2 oz) drained sun-dried tomatoes in oil, with enough oil from the jar to make a smooth paste.

TECHNIQUE

Stir-fry the rice in the butter for 1-2 minutes until all the grains are glossy.

FRESH PASTA WITH ASPARAGUS AND PARMESAN

Making fresh pasta is much easier than many people imagine and the flavour is far superior to that of many shop-bought fresh pastas, which can taste floury and be unpleasantly chewy. The initial expense of a pasta machine is soon forgotten as the results of homemade pasta become apparent. If you haven't time to make your own fresh pasta then I would recommend dried pasta as the better alternative: you will need 350 g (12 oz) dried tagliatelle.

SERVES 4

PASTA

225 g (8 oz) type '00' pasta flour

5 ml (1 tsp) salt

2 eggs, plus 1 egg yolk (all size 3)

15 ml (1 tbsp) extra-virgin olive oil

15 ml (1 tbsp) cold water

TO ASSEMBLE

225 g (8 oz) asparagus, trimmed

125 g (4 oz) unsalted butter

2 garlic cloves, peeled and sliced

60 ml (4 tbsp) chopped fresh parsley

50 g (2 oz) freshly grated Parmesan cheese

pepper

PREPARATION TIME
30 minutes, plus resting
COOKING TIME
6-8 minutes
FREEZING
Not suitable

585 CALS PER SERVING

1. To make the pasta, sift the flour and salt into a bowl. Make a well in the centre and add the eggs and egg yolk, oil and water. Gradually work into the flour to form a soft dough. Knead lightly for 3-4 minutes until smooth. Wrap in cling film and leave to rest for 30 minutes.

2. Divide the pasta dough into 8 pieces and pat flat. Pass each piece twice through each setting of the pasta machine, from the widest through to the narrowest, to form long thin sheets of pasta. Cut each sheet in half crosswise and hang over a clean pole as you go. Leave to rest for 5 minutes.

3. Next pass each sheet through the tagliatelle cutter attachment on the pasta machine and again hang the noodles over the pole as you go. Curl each group of noodles into 'nests' and place on a floured tea-towel.

4. Bring a large saucepan of water to the boil. At the same time, steam the asparagus for 3 minutes until just tender; drain, and cut into 5 cm (2 inch) lengths. Meanwhile heat the butter with the garlic in a small pan and cook over a medium heat until it starts to turn brown. Immediately remove from the heat.

5. Add 10 ml (2 tsp) salt to the pasta water. Plunge in the noodles, return to the boil and cook for 2-3 minutes until *al dente* (tender but firm to the bite). Immediately drain and return the pasta to the pan. Add the asparagus, parsley, butter and half the Parmesan, and toss gently.

6. Serve at once, topped with the remaining Parmesan and plenty of black pepper.

NOTE: Pasta flour is available from Italian delicatessens and some of the larger supermarkets. If you do not have a pasta machine, roll out the dough very thinly and cut into strips.

TECHNIQUE

Curl each group of noodles into 'nests' and place on a floured tea-towel.

INDEX

If you would like further information about the **Good Housekeeping Cookery Club**, please write to:
Penny Smith, Ebury Press, Random House, 20 Vauxhall Bridge Road, London SW1V 2SA.